DARE TO BE different!

101 Unconventional Careers

Polly Bird

Hodder & Stoughton
A MEMBER OF THE HODDER HEADLINE GROUP

To James, Paul and Rebecca - may they dare to be different.

Acknowledgements

Many people from the organisations mentioned in this book gave freely of information and advice about their careers. I thank them all and hope they will forgive me for not mentioning individuals by name. Judging by their kindness, it would be a pleasure to work in any of these jobs.

My thanks also to Charles Knight at Hodder and Stoughton and my agent Teresa Chris for their continuing encouragement. My husband Jon deserves thanks as always for his love and support.

Polly Bird

Orders: please contact Bookpoint Ltd, 39 Milton Park, Abingdon, Oxon OX14 4TD. Telephone: (44) 01235 400414, Fax: (44) 01235 400454. Lines are open from 9.00 – 6.00, Monday to Saturday, with a 24 hour message answering service. Email address: orders@bookpoint.co.uk

British Library Cataloguing in Publication Data
A catalogue record for this title is available from The British Library

ISBN 0 340 75360 9

First published 1999
Impression number   10 9 8 7 6 5 4 3 2 1
Year   2005 2004 2003 2002 2001 2000 1999

Cartoons by Mark Cripps
Cover photo by Telegraph Colour Library
Printed in Great Britain for Hodder & Stoughton Educational, a division of Hodder Headline Plc, 338 Euston Road, London NW1 3BH, by Redwood Books Ltd, Trowbridge, Wiltshire.

Contents

Introduction

Picture yourself at work in ten years time. How do you see yourself? Taking part in the usual daily grind or doing exciting and fulfilling work, something a bit out of the ordinary?

As you are reading this book, I assume you are looking for a job with that extra something – work that will positively make you want to leap out of bed with anticipation each morning.

But choosing a career can be difficult, especially if you want to do something a bit different. Whether you are looking for your first job or are considering a change of direction, the available advice seems to point to the same examples.

Most careers advisors do their best to be helpful. But however encouraging the advice, the range of careers on offer might not be quite what you really want.

There is nothing boring about any career so long as it is something that you really *want* to do. But supposing the careers you have been told about don't seem to excite you. Or you just want something that bit different. Where can you find out about them?

This book is the one you should read. It describes 101 unusual or unconventional careers that you may not know about or might not have considered.

Some of them require no specific qualifications, and you learn the work on-the-job. Others need specialist training and/or a degree. But what they all have in common is that they are not the standard jobs that are traditionally recommended by careers advisors.

This book is an ideas generator. Each career is described in detail, and then cross-referenced to other careers in the book that might be of interest. Further related careers are also listed so that you can follow up an interest with further reading. But simply scanning through the book will spark off new ideas and send you in a totally new career direction. You might start to read about becoming a Blacksmith, for example, but skip a page and become more interested in the information about being a Butler - from horses to houses in one leap!

Use this book as a starting point for your career research. When you have got some ideas, contact the relevant organisations and ask for information or advice. If possible, visit or ask for work experience with someone doing the work you are interested in. There is nothing like hands-on experience to tell you whether the job is the one for you.

Some of these jobs may be the start of a lifelong career; others might be stepping stones on the way. Whichever they are, you can be sure they will make your life more exciting.

What kind of career?

Looking for a new career can be exciting but bewildering. You may possibly have a very good idea of the kind of job you want; on the other hand, you may know that you want to do something different, but not know exactly what that might be.

Work tends to fall into a number of categories. For example, you can work with your hands such as in art and craft work, work outdoors perhaps with animals, birds or plants, you can heal by training as a complementary medicine practitioner, you can entertain, perhaps as a comedian, you can compete, as in ballooning or horse racing, or you can serve in many capacities - anything from being a courier to being a croupier. The choice is huge.

First you need to make those basic choices. Work out into which categories you would like your work to fall. Apart from the ones mentioned above, consider whether you like working with your brain, working in arts or sciences, dealing with old or new things, working for yourself or being part of an organisation. By answering these questions and similar ones honestly, you will get a good idea of the kind of work that will interest you.

● **Indoors or outdoors?** One of your most basic choices will be whether to work indoors or out. Some people prefer to be outside in all weathers and don't mind the rain or wind that is rather more frequent than sun in Britain. On the other hand, you might prefer to work indoors. This is a fundamental choice and will make a difference to the careers you look at. For example, if you want to work outdoors you could look at jobs like shepherd, dry stone waller, or gamekeeper. Indoor work could include patent agent, reflexologist or indexer.

● **What are you really like?** Your own personality will also determine the kind of work you might enjoy. For example, are you:

- introvert or extrovert?
- patient or impatient?
- kind or brusque?
- a loner or gregarious?

- confident or shy?
- adventurous or steady?
- brave or nervous?
- predictable or unpredictable?

Take the first qualities in this list. If you are extrovert and like making people laugh, you could be a comedian. An introvert would be a cartoonist. Or are you predictable or unpredictable? If you are reading this book, then you certainly have a streak of unpredictability in you! But if you generally prefer to know what comes next, then being a gamekeeper or an ecologist is not the obvious career choice.

Write down an honest description of your personality. You will soon get a clear picture of the type of person you are. It is no good deciding to become a hot air balloonist if you have no taste for adventure!

● **Your likes and dislikes** Make a list of all the things you like doing and all those you don't. You want to do a *different* job, so don't be afraid to consider all kinds of likes and dislikes you might have. For example, you might like working with your hands and being outdoors but hate working with lots of people. Perhaps being a gardener, forest warden or gamekeeper might appeal, or perhaps a woodworker. But if you hate dogs, then working as a guide dog mobility instructor is not a sensible choice.

And *how* do you like to work? On one project at a time or many at once? If you enjoy keeping busy and like change, then maybe a graphologist or out-of-print bookfinder will fit the bill. Steady work on one project at a time might point you towards a saddler or musical instrument maker. Do you like coming up with ideas or do you prefer to do what others tell you? If you like to work to instruction, then why not be a locksmith; an ideas person could be an artist or blacksmith.

● **What skills do you have?** Be realistic about what skills you have and those which you can learn. Before you look for a career in this book, work out what skills you have now and, just as important, which of your skills you really like using. For example, it is no good being good with figures if you find using them boring. On the other hand, if you passionately want to learn how to throw pots but have never tried pottery, don't let that stop you learning about it.

Now list all your talents, skills and abilities. Don't leave anything out. The fact that you are a good listener and can drive a car might point you in the direction of complementary medicine as a practitioner who provides home visits.

Make the list of your skills as comprehensive as possible. For example, what practical skills do you have? Can you:

- drive a car?
- cook?
- cycle?

- swim?
- draw?
- use numbers?

Or are you:

- good with children?
- good with animals?

- efficient?
- a good organiser?

Don't miss out any skill or talent you have, even if it is only that you can make people laugh. Any or all of your talents could be the basis for a new, unusual job.

Now work out what you really *like* doing. Do you like:

- cooking?
- being with people?
- shopping?
- going for long walks?

Now, what would you like to learn? Have you always wanted to know how to:

- draw?
- throw a pot?
- climb a mountain?
- fly?
- understand the stars?
- tell fortunes?
- call a sheep dog?
- juggle?

Whatever you want to learn, don't give up until you've tried.

Once you are clear about what you can do and what you like, you will begin to get an idea of the kinds of work that will interest you.

You might find that in spite of wanting to learn a skill you have no aptitude for it. If that is the case, do not give up entirely. Find another way of working in your chosen field. For example, if you want to be a thatcher but have no head for heights, why not try a related trade such as dry stone walling or house painting?

- **How will you learn?** The type of job you take might depend on the kind of training you would prefer. Many of the careers mentioned in this book can be learnt by on-the-job training, either generally or as a carefully designed apprenticeship or traineeship. To train for other careers you might have to attend specific courses or obtain certain qualifications before you start.

Which type of training you prefer will depend on whether you learn best by watching more experienced people work or by listening and reading about the subject. In any case, there will always be more to learn and it will take several years before you are fully experienced.

Traditionally, many jobs were taught using the apprenticeship system. For several years, usually seven, beginners would work for and with masters of their trades and in return would be taught the necessary skills. When apprentices had learnt the trade they were qualified to practise it in their turn.

Nowadays the traditional apprenticeship system is drastically reduced or non-existent in many trades. Where it does still exist, it can be the best way to learn. Even where it does not exist, or in jobs where it never existed, learning by watching and working with an expert is a good idea. Children learn quickly by watching and imitating adults; so adults can learn by being taught by an expert.

So if you cannot find training in your chosen job, look around for someone who is already practising it. Ask if they will take you on as an apprentice or simply teach you. If you cannot afford to pay them, perhaps they would accept labour in return for teaching you. Many people are delighted to pass their skills and advice on. This is particularly so in trades which are dying for lack of new recruits.

If you are interested in a career which involves extensive academic training and you cannot afford it, see if there are alternatives. For example, if you like the idea of being a patent agent or cartographer, it is still possible to enter the profession without a degree and to work your way up. This may be a declining option but you can look into the possibility.

If finances are the problem, see what is available. Check with your local authority to see whether you are entitled to a grant. If not, ask the college or university whether there are any financial schemes for poor students. Investigate the student loan system or Career Development Loans. Perhaps the Open University has courses that would suit you and you could spread the cost over a number of years. Alternatively, adult education classes could get you started.

● **Is there a relevant organisation?** Whether you are just starting out on your career or are fully qualified, it is worth joining the relevant trade or industry organisation or a related club. This is particularly important with unusual careers, because such groups might be the only sources of available help. Sometimes you can only join the organisation once you are fully qualified, but often industry or professional organisations have a student or associate membership category. Equally, non-professional careers have related organisations that can be useful – for example, a classic car restorer might consider joining the relevant classic car club. Joining a relevant organisation can provide training, information, contacts, and sometimes professional kudos.

Members of clubs and professional organisations can be very helpful by giving advice, introducing you to others and by showing you how things are done. If you are looking for work experience, a master willing to take an apprentice, or advice about the right steps to take to your chosen career, then your first call should be to the relevant club or organisation.

This book provides as much information as possible about the careers concerned. But new organisations are forming all the time. Search out relevant organisations - they exist for practically every subject. Look at the *Directory of British Associations* published annually by CBD Research Ltd.

● **Employed or self-employed?** Many of the careers in this book can be pursued either as an employee or by becoming self-employed. Think carefully about the consequences of being self-employed. It might sound fun, but have you got the capital investment needed? - even small businesses need some money up front. You might need to investigate business loans. Are you prepared to do *everything*, including the bookkeeping? Can you put up with the loneliness and antisocial hours?

The best way might be to start as an employee and learn your trade before becoming self-employed. Learn your skills and build up your contacts and save enough capital to start, before setting up on your own.

Alternatively, start your new career as a hobby or work part-time until you are established. This has the advantage of allowing you to earn while you learn your craft. You might discover that you prefer to keep it as a part-time or subsidiary occupation. Also, if you find out that you are not as keen on the job as you thought, you have lost nothing and still have your main career to fall back on.

School or college leavers might not have the option of choosing part-time work, but it is possible to try out many careers and jobs at evening classes or at weekend workshops, this way you can decide whether you are interested enough to make a full-time career of it.

● **Take up the challenge** You are reading this book because you want to do something different. You don't want to be constrained by traditional career choices and predictable job patterns. You want a challenge and to be excited by the work you do.

Once you have decided what kind of work you would like to do and what skills you have, and have taken training and finances into account, read this book and make a choice. Don't be afraid to change your mind. If you look at shepherding but are suddenly fascinated by becoming a patent agent, then follow your heart. Find out about the work, see if you can talk to someone doing the job you want to pursue. Take the perks and problems into account. Then, if you are still keen, go ahead. It is *your* life, so make the most of it.

All jobs will require determination and hard work. But if you set your mind to it, you can do it. Have a go, and *Dare to Be Different!*

Read this first!

Where an organisation has a Website it is courteous to look at that first. It will often give you all the information you need. You can then ask follow-up questions by e-mail. If you do need to write or phone, you will not need to ask questions that the site has already answered.

Always enclose a stamped self-addressed envelope (SAE) when you write to any organisation in this book. Many smaller organisations cannot respond to you unless you do so. This is in any case a courtesy. Any phone calls you make should be short and to the point.

The information given in this book is as up-to-date as possible at the time of going to press and is given in good faith. Before committing yourself to any job, make sure that you have the most recent information by contacting the relevant organisations and reading the recent literature. The best way to find out what any job involves is to do appropriate voluntary or work experience or to take a relevant short course.

The guide to earnings is in all cases approximate. Remember that there is now a minimum wage – currently £3 per hour for people aged 18-21 and £3.60 per hour for those aged 21 and over.

Addresses for careers in the 'Find out about' sections are listed alphabetically at the end of the book.

Earnings guide

£ Under £5000 per year

£ £ £6–10,000 per year

£ £ £ £11–15,000 per year

£ £ £ £ £16–20,000 per year

£ £ £ £ £ £20,000+ per year

Alternative medicine practitioner £ £ £ £

Whether you call them alternative or complementary medicines, these normally exist outside the traditional health service practices. However, more and more GPs and hospitals are realising the value of alternative and complementary medicines and some alternative medical practitioners are connected to surgeries or have patients referred to them by hospitals.

Alternative practices range from homeopathy to herbal medicine, acupuncture, Alexander Technique and many others. Some now have professional status and practitioners must be registered with the appropriate organisation. Others have a more flexible approach and can be learnt by anyone with enough enthusiasm and determination. However, as you will be dealing with other people's health, it is wise to train and register with one of the relevant organisations.

As an alternative medical practitioner you can work full- or part-time or be self-employed. You can also choose whether to set up your own practice at home, in special offices, or work in an already established practice. You can even choose to take your skills on house calls.

You do not normally need any traditional medical training and this is an attractive proposition. However, more and more GPs are completing training in disciplines such as acupuncture to supplement their traditional skills.

You do need to like people and to be prepared to learn your skills from a recognised practitioner, that is someone who has been properly trained and practising for several years. Once you have completed the appropriate training course you are eligible for membership of the relevant professional associations. For lists of alternative and complementary medicine organisations and information about practitioners in your preferred therapy contact one of the organisations listed below.

• How many alternative medicine practitioners are there?
It is impossible to say because not all practitioners belong to a recognised professional organisation.

• Job prospects and pay
The job prospects do fluctuate depending on which alternative therapies are currently in vogue. Also, if like many practitioners you are self-employed, your income will vary. But with determination and dedication you can earn a living wage. Your average hourly charges are likely to be between £25 and £40.

• Start-up costs
These depend on the alternative therapy you are practising and whether you are setting up a separate practice or starting from your own home. You might need a couch or the medicines you will use.

- **How old must you be?** There is usually no specific age limit although it is unlikely that patients will trust you to treat them if you are under 18. The various alternative medicine organisations have their own rules about the age for entry and training. You will also need insurance and 18 is the minimum age you can acquire it.

- **Training** The training depends on which alternative therapy you want to practice. You can teach yourself some things such as homeopathy or herbal medicine, but in virtually all cases it is important to be trained by a practising professional, either on a recognised course or as an individual pupil of an experienced practitioner. Courses range in length from one day and weekend tasters to longer full-time courses lasting up to a year. For some complementary medicine professions such as chiropractic or osteopathy you might need to undertake full-time training for up to five years. In some cases distance learning courses are also available.

- **Qualifications** You do not necessarily need a qualification, although it is possible to gain certificates and diplomas in most therapies. Some disciplines now require all practitioners to have a qualification recognised by the relevant professional body. In any case your patients will be more reassured that you will treat them safely and effectively if you have a qualification from the recognised professional organisation.

Contacts: Always enclose an A5 SAE when contacting these organisations. *British Complementary Medicine Association*, 249 Fosse Road South, Leicester LE3 1AE; *The Institute for Complementary Medicine,* ICM, PO Box 194, London SE16 1QZ. Tel: 020-7237 5165. Fax: 020-7237 5175; *Council for Complementary & Alternative Medicine,* 206 Latimer Road, London W10. Tel: 020-8968 3862. For information about particular branches of alternative or complimentary medicine look at the advertisements at the back of magazines like *Here's Health.*

See also: Chiropractor, reflexologist, trichologist.
Find out about: Herbalist, Alexander Technique, dental assistant, masseur/se.

Antiques dealer   £ – £ £ £ £ £ £

Your local bric a brac shop is not technically dealing in antiques because antiques are normally classified as over 100 years old. But as people can collect anything that takes their fancy you could be dealing with more modern things - the 'antiques of the future'.

Antiques dealers buy and sell antiques with the aim of making a profit. This can be done through anything from a market stall to auctioning valuable items at major auction houses such as Sotheby's or Christies.

You will do better if you specialise in one aspect of antiques, for example in furniture, paintings or silver. By learning as much as you can about the area you have chosen you will be better placed to recognise an item's real value and its possible profit potential.

You need to have a good eye for a bargain and an acute business sense because this is a career where people will try to take you for a ride. You also need to be able to get on with people, as part of your ability to get a good deal will depend on your personal powers of persuasion.

● **How many antiques dealers are there?** Many smaller dealers are not members of the main trade organisations so it is impossible to estimate numbers.

● **Job prospects and pay** Most antiques businesses are small and there is a lot of competition in the trade.

● **Start-up costs** These will depend on whether you want to start with a stall in a market or set up your own shop. Either way you will need to put in a great deal of financial investment for premises and stock. Your capital outlay could be considerable depending on the size of business you want to run.

● **How old must you be?** There are no specific age limits and indeed some people help at antiques market stalls at quite a young age.

● **Training** Learn as much as you can about antiques by visiting museums, art galleries and stately homes, by reading books, visiting auctions and making contacts. Help out at a junk stall or get a weekend job in a local antique shop. Get a job in a local auction room to get to know the names, construction and auction price of items.

● **Qualifications** You don't need any qualifications unless you want to work in a top auction house in which case you will need a degree, preferably in Art history.

Contacts: *The British Antique Dealers Association*, 20 Rutland Gate, London SW7 1BD. Tel: 020-7589 4128. Fax: 020-7581 9083.

See also: Out-of-print book finder, auctioneer.
Find out about: Art dealer, second-hand bookseller.

Archaeologist

A love of the past and an enthusiasm for detective work might make you the ideal archaeologist. Archaeology is the study of the physical remains and environmental effects of human behaviour. The time span is enormous, ranging from the origins of humans millions of years ago to such things as industrial remains in the twentieth century. As a detective of the past you might be studying the remains of cities, human bones, plant remains, ancient metals and textiles, prehistoric tombs, in fact anything that gives us an insight into our own history. Although you might think that archaeology only deals with periods when there were no written records, it also supplements periods for which written records remain.

Archaeology as a subject has links with many other subjects so whatever your special interest you will find that archaeology can have a use for you.

The popular image of an archaeologist is of someone digging away at the earth in a trench in a field in the middle of nowhere. It is true that this *can* be part of your work, but there are many other jobs in archaeology. You might be interested in conservation, illustration, aerial photography, surveying, compiling archaeological computer databases, studying biological remains, teaching - the variety is tremendous. The Council for British Archaeology (*CBA*) website is particularly informative.

The work can be full- or part-time and self-employed archaeologists do exist although there are not so many as there used to be. Much work is connected with museums.

- **How many archaeologists are there?** About 4500.

- **Job prospects and pay** There are more qualified people wanting jobs in archaeology than there are jobs to go round. In 1997 there were only 176 jobs advertised in archaeology and about 300 new graduates look for a job in the profession each year. Unless you are lucky enough to get a job with a national agency such as *English Heritage*, a local authority or a museum, you will find that the work tends to be short term and with limited job prospects. Your salary won't be large so you need to love the subject. You can find out about digs that take volunteers by reading the CBAs *Briefing* which appears in alternate months to its magazine *British Archaeology*. For jobs contact the *Institute of Field Archaeologists* which runs a job information service. The average starting salary is £12,327 and the national average is £19,167.

- **Start-up costs** Most archaeologists involved in field work like to have their own pointing trowel which will cost a few pounds. Apart from that there are no specific start-up costs as all tools should be supplied by whoever employs you.

- **How old must you be?** The *Council for British Archaeology (CBA)* has a *Young Archaeologists Club* for members aged 9-16. There is no standard minimum age but many excavations may only be able to accept people over 18. To study archaeology at university you need to be 18 or over.

- **Training** You can get practical training as a volunteer on special training digs although these might charge a fee. Most people working in archaeology have a degree either in archaeology or a related discipline.

- **Qualifications** The preferred qualification is a degree, **but** there are also NVQs and SVQs in practical museum work and part-time certificates and diplomas in archaeology.

Contacts: (NB enclose an SAE) *Council for British Archaeology*, Bowes Morrell House, 111 Walmgate, York YO1 9WA. Website: **www.britarch.ac.uk/index.html**

See also: Stonemason, genealogist, private detective.
Find out about: Museum worker, local government heritage officer.

Artists' model   £

The one thing you *don't* need as an artists' model is a beautiful body. Anyone who is prepared to sit naked in front of artists, whether a group of students or a professional artist, is welcome. Some people make it a full-time career, but most models work part-time. Many models use the job as a way of supplementing their main career - models come from all backgrounds. Most models work in art schools for student groups.

You will normally expect to have a screen to change behind or a room. You then emerge with a wrap or coat on to keep you warm while the students get their materials ready. You will then be asked to pose in particular ways by the teacher or be told to choose a suitable position, e.g. lying, standing. Poses might last from five minutes to a couple of hours with breaks. You need to be able to keep still for about half an hour at a time so it helps if you like thinking your own thoughts! Sometimes you might be asked to move slowly or stand in poses for a minute at a time and then move.

During the breaks you can have a hot drink and wander around to see what pictures the students have made of you - not always a flattering experience!

If you want to be employed by practising artists you could contact them directly. But make sure that you check their credentials and if necessary take a friend with you to chaperone.

● **How many artists' models are there?** Nobody knows how many models there are - each art school will have a number of regular models it calls on.

● **Job prospects and pay** As long as there is a need for a model you can go on working. Models can continue working into old age. The pay is hourly.

● **How old must you be?** It is unusual to employ models under the age of 17 and there is no upper age limit.

● **Training** No training is needed.

● **Qualifications** The only qualifications are patience and a lack of embarrassment.

Contacts: Phone your local art schools, further education colleges or adult education institutions for vacancies.

See also: Circus performer, Tai Chi teacher.
Find out about: Artist, hairdresser.

Astrologer   £ – £ £ £ £ £

Astrologers use the date and place of birth to consult the planets for information on their clients' lives, and provide an analysis of their future. This is done by personal consultation, written report or oral cassette.

Once you have the client's details you draw up a chart of the heavens showing the position of the planets at the time - usually the time of birth, but other important dates may be used. This is usually done by hand, but nowadays computers are frequently used. You then read the chart to discover the planetary influences at work on your client's life and write a report about your findings. You might be asked to calculate charts for famous people, pets or even fictional characters.

Unless you become a well-known name you are unlikely to be given your own column. You will often find that journalists used to produce the 'stars' page. Most astrologers, even if writing for a newspaper or magazine, will be self-employed.

• **How many astrologers are there?** This is difficult to estimate because many people practise astrology among their family and friends, and others are part-time. There are about 5000 members of the various astrological groups, but not all of them are practising astrologers. There might be about 300-400 semi-professional or professional astrologers.

● **Job prospects and pay** This depends on how hard you want to work. Most astrologers supplement their income by more traditional work. However, the prospects for part-time work are great. There are very few full-time astrologers and few reach the heights of media astrologers such as Russell Grant or Mystic Meg. As a professional astrologer expect to earn most of your income through writing for newspapers and magazines, writing books and giving personal readings. Most astrologers are self-employed and part-time and only a few manage the heady heights of full-time employment on a newspaper or magazine.

● **Start-up costs** Basic business costs, an answer machine, and the cost of any training. You also need to buy a computer for writing reports and articles. Some astrologers use computers for drawing up charts since it is sometimes quicker and more cost effective than drawing by hand. A computer costs from about £1000-1500 and a printer and software suitable for a professional astrologer will cost another £300. You will get most of your clients by recommendation so join one of the astrological organisations and apply for consultancy status when eligible. Your name will then be sent regularly to media organisations.

● **How old must you be?** There is no age limit.

● **Training** You can teach yourself from books and many people do. There is nothing stopping you setting up as an astrologer and charging for your services. However, you will impress your customers more if you get recognised training. In many local areas you will find short courses available at evening classes or adult education classes. The *Faculty of Astrological Studies* is the main training body and there are five approved schools. The Faculty also provides correspondence courses and arranges Saturday schools. Courses cost between £250 and £290 and seminars cost £35 each. If you specialise in a branch of astrology such as medicine or financial advice you will need appropriate training. You need a good command of English and also a good general education including maths because astrology examinations require an understanding of logarithms. Counselling techniques are also a bonus, and these can be obtained through the *Faculty of Astrological Studies*, the main teaching body for astrology. The *British Astrological and Psychic Society (BAPS)* provides a two-part certificated correspondence course in Astrology accredited by the *Advisory Panel for Astrological Education*

(APAE). A tutored course is also available. Send a SAE to their address below. Alternatively you can arrange for private tuition.

● **Qualifications** None are needed, but nowadays your clients will expect to see some formal qualification. A certificate course can take from three months to a year to complete depending on whether it is an evening or correspondence course. This will teach you basic astrology and how to complete a chart manually (although most astrologers now use computers). You can then take a diploma through one of the approved astrology schools. BAPS will test you for consultancy status through a written exam and four vettings. This is suitable if you have studied astrology on your own and have been practising for a number of years.

Contacts: *Faculty of Astrological Studies*, BM7470, London WC1N 3XX. Tel: 07000-790 143. Fax: 01689-603537. E-mail: info@astrology.org.uk. Website: **www.astrology.org.uk**; *BAPS Astrology School*, 51 Roche Way, Wellingborough, Northamptonshire NN8 5YE. Tel: 01933-401158; *BAPS National Secretary*, Robert Denholm House, Bletchingly Road, Nutfield, Surrey RH1 4HW. E-mail: BAPS@tlpplc.com

See also: Genealogist, graphologist, Feng Shui consultant.
Find out about: Palm reader, tarot reader.

Astronomer   £ £ £ £

Patrick Moore is probably the best known popular astronomer. Someone who spends his time gazing at stars and planets and has a vast knowledge of the sky. Or else you might think of people in white coats in observatories looking through vast telescopes. But astronomy is a subject with varied work.

Astronomy is the study of phenomena occurring outside the earth. An astronomer's work is theoretical and observational, but nowadays the amount of time you will spend 'star gazing' is quite small. Infrared or radio telescopes and satellite probes feed data back to computers so looking through a telescope at the sky is now not as necessary as before.

Observations are made at night from telescopes all over the UK and either space or ground based facilities, but the measurements from a few hours' observations might take several months to analyse. To analyse the data you need to be able to use advanced maths and computer techniques. The work involves the handling of vast amounts of data.

Virtually all astronomers also work in research departments in universities or government departments or government-funded observatories. However, you might get work designing instruments for observers. Most astronomers are graduates or postgraduates, but there are opportunities for a small number of support staff such as technicians or administrators.

● **Job prospects and pay** As most astronomers will find work in the research departments of universities you will need to find financial support either through a studentship through a Research Council, university or industry. Employment prospects are as good as those for other PhD graduates. Most jobs are on short-term contracts.

Amateur astronomers can contribute to the profession by writing up their observations or by giving talks. But this is unlikely to provide a living wage - unless you are the next Patrick Moore!

● **Start-up costs** To start up you need only buy a telescope, the price of which will vary with size and the strength of the lens.

● **How old must you be?** The normal age limits for first and higher degrees apply. Amateurs can start at any age.

● **Training** You can learn by observation and from books, lectures and societies. However, to qualify as an astronomer you need a first degree in a relevant subject such as maths, geology, physics, chemistry, computer science or statistics. You will then go on to a higher degree. In astronomy all jobs in research departments require a doctorate (PhD), but support roles can be obtained with a first degree.

● **Qualifications** Although amateurs can do well if they have the ability to write and pass their knowledge on, the main route is through a first degree followed by a doctorate. Technicians and administrators can get a job with anything from 4 GCSEs to a degree, depending on the work involved.

Tel: 020-7734 4582. Fax: 020-7734 3307. E-mail: mail_ras@star.ucl.ac.uk.

See also: Cartographer, naval architect, fingerprint officer.
Find out about: Geographer, biologist, physicist.

Auctioneer   £££ – ££££

If you like the sound of your own voice, can speak quickly but clearly, are quick witted and like to control what goes on around you then perhaps auctioneering is the job for you. Whether selling farm livestock or a Rembrandt, an auctioneer needs to be constantly alert and scrupulously honest.

There are four general types of auctioneer. There are those who specialise in property and who work for one of about a dozen major firms. Then there are the plant auctioneers who auction machinery, factories and so on. There are also agricultural auctioneers who deal in livestock. The last branch of auctioneering is fine arts and chattels ('anything not nailed down'). Christies and Sotheby's are the major and respected firms in this area, but there are also unqualified and unregulated auctioneers in this area who deal from church halls and the like and often deal with things like house clearances. You should aim to be an honest and respected auctioneer.

● **How many auctioneers are there?** As auctioneers do not have to belong to any specific organisation, their number is unknown. However, there are fewer working in the areas of properties and plant than in agriculture. There are thousands of unqualified auctioneers dealing in chattels.

● **Job prospects and pay** At the unqualified end of the job your prospects and pay are poor. The better qualified you are the more likely you are to be taken on by a reputable firm who will encourage further training and qualifications. The better your qualifications and experience the better your pay. A partner in an auction house can earn 'a fortune'. A graduate surveyor who has not yet got his or her letters can expect to earn about £12-15,000.

● **Start-up costs** You don't need a trading licence but you might need to pay for a licence or be registered in order to sell certain kinds of goods. It is obviously advisable to hold Professional Indemnity Insurance. You also have to provide notices displaying your name conspicuously in whatever place you are holding the auction.

- **How old must you be?** There is no age limit, but training schemes and jobs with firms mean that 18 is the usual minimum age.

- **Training** You do not need any training to be an auctioneer and anyone can set up as one. However, many auctioneers do belong to one of the main professional bodies such as *The Incorporated Society of Valuers and Auctioneers (ISVA), Association of Livestock Auctioneers* or similar. Unlike many other auctioneer professional organisations the ISVA is an examining body and has a rigorous training programme. It insists on a strict code of conduct for its members. It also has strict rules about handling clients' money and insists that all its members hold professional indemnity insurance. Qualification allows members to work in areas other than auctioneering, such as valuation.

   You might find a small firm of auctioneers who would be willing to take you on and train you in-house, but this is more difficult nowadays.

19

• Qualifications

Many auctioneers are unregulated so there are no specific qualifications. However, it is clearly sensible to join one of the professional organisations mentioned above and to take advantage of their expertise and advice. Take part in training programmes where possible if you want to serve your customers well and to stay within the law. Qualification will also improve your career prospects.

Contacts: *The Incorporated Society of Valuers and Auctioneers (ISVA)*, 3 Cadogan Gate, London SW1X 0AS Tel: 020-7235 2282. Fax: 020-7235 4390. E-mail: hq@isva.co.uk; *Central Association of Agricultural Valuers*, Market Chambers, 35 Market Place, Coleford, Gloucestershire GL16 8AA. Tel: 01549-832979. Fax: 01549-810701. E-mail: enquire@caav.org.uk. Website: **www.caav.org.uk/**

See also: Comedian, tour guide.
Find out about: Actor, salesperson.

Bailiff   £ £ – £ £ £

You have the choice of becoming one of three types of bailiff: a sheriff's officer, county court bailiff or private bailiff. Each kind of bailiff is responsible for enforcing court orders for debt, recovering goods, repossessing property and making civil arrests. In England and Wales a legal document can be personally served by any adult without the need to have a professional qualification. Sheriff's officers are officers of the court but are actually private sector bailiffs with a monopoly to enforce high court judgements in their area. County court bailiffs are salaried civil servants employed by The Court Service. Private bailiffs are the largest branch of the profession and about three quarters of them carry a certificate issued by a judge to allow them to enforce certain types of debt.

The Northern Ireland Enforcement Office carries out all enforcement in the province. It directly employs the bailiffs who are civil servants. In Scotland there are sheriff's officers.

Bailiffs have a reputation for 'bullying', but this is usually unfounded. The nature of their job, i.e. collecting debts, and the fact that most of these are collected by private bailiffs means that legal action seems unpleasant. You do need to be able to get on with people in what are difficult and sometimes unpleasant circumstances, but at the same time be assertive enough to follow necessary action through. Private bailiffs should not be confused with creditors' agents who have no power to remove goods and no immunities but who call on debtors to intimidate them into paying.

You can be a bailiff simply by doing the job and thus get the rights and immunities. It is usual to combine working as a bailiff with other work because the pay is low. Some bailiffs are also auctioneers.

● **How many bailiffs are there?** There are 2000 private bailiffs in England and Wales, and this is the largest sector of the profession.

● **Job prospects and pay** Private bailiffs and sheriff's officers are in the private sector and pay varies between firms. You can expect to earn a straight salary of between £9-15,000. It is common to get a basic salary of £8000 and a percentage of the enforcement fees you recover. Many bailiffs are sole practitioners and live on the fees they recover from debtors and the little the government creditors pay for abortive action. County Court Bailiffs are civil servants and get civil service pay rates.

● **Start-up costs** The usual costs are for starting a small business requiring office equipment - telephone, fax, etc. You should also pay for professional indemnity. A car is essential and you might need to hire a van for removals in perhaps two percent of cases.

● **How old must you be?** You must be 18 or over.

● **Training** County Court Bailiffs are trained, but otherwise anybody can be a bailiff if you can persuade someone to give you the work.

● **Qualifications** You don't need any qualifications although if you wish you can take exams with the *Certificated Bailiffs Association of England & Wales* or the *Society of Messengers-at-Arms & Sheriffs' Officers*. For some debts a private bailiff needs a certificate issued by a circuit judge under the distress for rent rules. These rules might be tightened in the near future.

Contacts: *Certificated Bailiffs Association of England & Wales*, Ridgefield House, 14 John Dalton Street, Manchester M2 6JR; *Society of Messengers-at-Arms & Sheriffs' Officers*, 21 Ainslie Place, Edinburgh EH3 6AJ. Tel: 0131-225 9110. Fax: 0131-220 3468.

See also: Croupier, gamekeeper.
Find out about: Police officer, traffic warden, security guard.

Bee keeper   £ – £ £

Small scale production of natural high quality food is in demand and it is possible to make a living out of bee keeping for the production of honey. However, it is hard work and stressful and you have to be prepared to work all the year round. Bee keeping will take about half an hour of your time per hive each week from mid April to August. In addition you extract honey twice a year. One hive can produce 60lb (27kg) in a good season although an average hive would produce about 27-30lb (113kg) surplus.

You buy hives and bees and then look after the bees and eventually harvest the honey. Bees extract nectar form flowers, mix it with enzymes and store it in wax honeycombs until water level is reduced. The cell is then capped with a thin layer of wax until needed. When the capping is done you know that the honey is ready for harvesting. You can then lift out the boxes containing the honeycomb and extract the honey in a machine called a spinner. You need to wear protective clothing while opening a hive although bees will not normally sting if unprovoked. Because bee keeping has traditionally been important to rural economies there are many superstitions surrounding bees. The best known is that you should tell them about any death in the family.

Bees are susceptible to disease so sometimes whole areas of the country lose their bees and therefore the investment in them.

You need to check that you can meet all the financial and legal obligations for keeping bees and preparing and selling honey, including any European Commission directives.

Get as much advice from experts as possible and consult your local *Training and Enterprise Agency (TEC)*.

● **How many bee keepers are there?** There are no accurate figures because many bee keepers operate on a small scale and do not belong to an organisation.

● **Start-up costs** Clothing and tools cost about £100 and good second-hand hives with bees cost about £35-50 each. If you want to make a living you will need to be prepared to invest money in the project, although you can start with one hive and acquire more as you make a profit.

• **How old must you be?** Any age.

• **Training** The best training is to work with an experienced bee keeper and to research the subject as widely as possible. You might also be able to learn more at your local agricultural college.

• **Qualifications** You don't need any qualifications, but you do need to learn a lot about bee keeping.

Contacts: *British Isles Beekeeper Association (BBKA)*, National Agriculture Centre, Stoneleigh, Warwickshire CV8 2LZ. Fax: 01203-690682. E-mail: sallyedwards@bbka.demon.co.uk. Website: **www.bbka.demon.co.uk/index.htm**; *Bee Improvement and Bee Breeders Association*, Website: **www.angus.co.uk/bibba/**; *The Rural Development Commission*, 141 Castle Street, Salisbury, Wiltshire SP1 3TP. Tel: 01722-336255. Fax: 01722-332769.

See also: Fish farmer, shepherd.
Find out about: Goat farmer, herb grower.

Bird sanctuary warden   £ £ – £ £ £

Becoming a warden is a very popular job with people who love the outdoor life and want to contribute in a practical way to wildlife conservation.

As a warden with *The Royal Society for the Protection of Birds* (RSPB) you would work with conservation officers and countryside rangers to maintain land and biological records, monitor species and habitats and maintain visitor policy on the RSPB reserves. You would become part of the local community by giving talks and assisting farmers.

You need a sound education, a broad, practical knowledge of birds and natural history. You also need to be a good manager and to be prepared to tackle all kinds of jobs from looking after staff and talking to visitors to clearing a ditch or counting wildfowl. There is a lot of administration work too so a warden's job is not just watching birds.

Your life as a bird sanctuary warden is varied and interesting - and hard work! For example, you will be involved in the everyday maintenance care and guiding work at the site, but you might also take part in surveys of a bird species or the protection of a protected species. The work varies from one reserve to another. You might be doing practical habitat management such as coppicing or building hides, survey work or work with visitors such as running information centres, or leading guided talks. The work can be physically demanding, but not all your time will be spent out of doors. The work varies according to the weather and the seasons. You need to be a good, all-round manager.

To become a warden you must start off by becoming a volunteer. It is only by regular volunteering over a long period of time that you can show your aptitude and keenness for the work. In the *RSPB* it is a natural progression to move from being a regular volunteer to being a seasonal contract warden.

- **How many bird sanctuary wardens are there?** A minimum number is the 100 short-term contract wardens employed by the RSPB.

- **Job prospects and pay** Most employment is on a contract basis so don't expect long term stability, at least to start with. Wardening vacancies are scarce. The RSPB takes on seasonal contract staff for periods from three months to a year and these jobs are sometimes offered to reliable, talented volunteers. The pay is not high compared with other professions with a similar level of responsibility. Vacancies for wardens' jobs are generally advertised in the natural history journals such as the *RSPB*'s *Birds* and the environmental sections of papers such as *The Guardian*.

- **Start-up costs** None.

- **How old must you be?** You can be a voluntary warden with the *RSPB* from the age of 16. Accommodation is provided, but you need to provide your own food and pocket money. A voluntary warden must be prepared to work for a minimum of one week. Apply to the Reserves Department of the RSPB. Employment as a seasonal warden is unlikely until you are 18 or over.

- **Training** Volunteering first is vital and you will learn much on the job. As a volunteer you might also get the chance to get a City & Guilds qualification in Countryside Care and Conservation as well as practical experience and contacts. The *British Trust for Conservation Volunteers (BTCV)* also takes volunteers and trains them in practical skills. You should improve your knowledge of birds by joining the *RSPB*, your local Wildlife Trust and by subscribing to good wildlife magazines. The RSPB has junior sections.

- **Qualifications** Even though the job is largely practical you need sound academic qualifications. You should have a broad range of GCSEs (or Scottish Standard Grades) with good grades including English and maths. You may also need A levels or Scottish Higher Grades which might include subjects like zoology, botany, applied biology, biology, geography, maths, economics and statistics. If you decide to take an HND or degree choose relevant courses. You also need a broad knowledge of birds and natural history.

Contacts: The RSPB or BTCV can provide opportunities for volunteering. When you have enough experience, look for jobs advertised by the environmental organisations in the local and national press. Although the RSPB advertises many jobs internally it is willing to consider external applicants for them. So if you know someone working in the RSPB ask them to look out for suitable jobs that arise. Also try the specialist press such as *The Countryside Jobs Service*.
RSPB, The Lodge, Sandy, Bedfordshire SG19 2DL. Tel: 01767-680551. Fax: 01767-692365. Website: **www.rspb.co.uk**; BTCV (British Trust for Conservation Volunteers), 36 St Mary's Street, Wallingford, Oxfordshire OX10 0EU. Tel: 01491-839766. Fax: 01491-839646. E-mail: information@btcv.org.uk. Website: **www.btcv.org.uk**.

See also: Shepherd, gamekeeper.
Find out about: Ornithologist, zoologist, zoo worker.

Blacksmith and farrier   £ £ – £ £ £

Blacksmiths are not to be confused with farriers who specialise in shoeing horses and ponies. Farriers examine horses hooves and diagnose their needs according to the conditions in which the animals work. However, they do use blacksmithing skills to make their nails and shoes by hand and often make their own tools and do blacksmithing work and agricultural repairs. They can also visit their customers, taking their equipment with them. Only farriers can legally shoe horses. Some farriers are also farmers.

Blacksmiths traditionally produced ironwork and agricultural machinery. Although there are blacksmiths who work in forges, there are also those who are employed in industry - making things that can still only be made by hand.

Blacksmiths work with metals and still use the traditional materials of a furnace and anvil, but they also use modern technology such as power presses and hammers, oxyacetylene and electronic arc lamps. Nowadays you are more likely to be producing decorative ironwork such as ornate gates or lanterns. You will work with a variety of metals mainly mild steel, but also wrought iron, stainless steel, copper, brass and bronze. You cut metal to shape from drawings and then heat the metal over an open coke, coal or gas fire until it is pliable and can be shaped on an anvil by blows from a hammer or other tools.

If you want to be a blacksmith you will need to find yourself a master blacksmith who will train you. Working as an apprentice is still the best way to learn the trade. Unfortunately, there are few traditional blacksmiths left so you will have to ask around. Perhaps your nearest farm employs one on a freelance basis.

Modern artist blacksmiths often train at art school and choose blacksmithing as a form of art or craft. You can branch out from the craft to become involved in architecture, design or design education.

- **How many blacksmiths are there?** There are about 600 artist blacksmiths in the UK.

- **Job prospects and pay** An apprentice's wages will depend on the conditions of the apprenticeship.

- **Start-up costs** You will need to buy your tools and metals and rent a work space.

- **How old must you be?** 16+

- **Training** You can train as a farrier by being apprenticed to an approved training farrier. This takes four years. Some artist blacksmiths go to art school. Some colleges provide courses in art blacksmithing. There are also private courses run by individuals. Look at the *BABA* (*British Artist Blacksmiths Association*) website for details.

- **Qualifications** You don't need any qualifications to be a farrier or blacksmith, but you might find art training useful to be an artist black-smith. To work as a farrier you must complete your apprenticeship and pass the Diploma of the *Worshipful Company of Farriers* and then register with its registration Council. You do need to be physically strong, have stamina and an eye for design, and have some knowledge of structural engineering.

Contacts: *The Farriers Registration Council*, Sefton House, Adam Court, Newark Road, Peterborough PE1 5PP. Tel: 01733-319911; *The Worshipful Company of Blacksmiths*, The Clerk, 27 Cheyne Walk, Grange Park, London N21 1DB. Tel: 020-8364 1522; *National Association of Farriers, Blacksmiths and Agricultural Engineers*, Avenue R, Seventh Street, NAC, Stoneleigh, Kenilworth CV8 2LG. Tel: 01203-696595; *British Artist Blacksmiths Association*, Lyndhurst, Carlton Husthwaite, Thirsk, North Yorkshire YO7 2BJ. Website: **www.baba.org.uk/**; *Herefordshire College of Technology*, Folly Lane, Hereford HR1 1LS. Tel: 01432-352235. Fax: 01432-365357. E-mail: enquiries@htc.herefordshire.com. Website: **www.htc.herefordshire.com**.

See also: Locksmith, stonemason.
Find out about: Gardener, engineer.

Bookbinder

A beautifully bound book is not only a work of art but something that will give lasting practical use and pleasure. If you love books and are good with your hands then bookbinding might be just the job you are looking for.

Bookbinders repair pages, spines or whole books and can decorate the covers either with simple lettering or by using gold leaf. There are a number of different styles of bookbinding, for example, full or quarter binding, and the binding material can be leather, cloth, paper, vellum or silk. An enterprising bookbinder can also bind books in unusual modern materials such as plastic! Artist-bookbinders can create a work of art out of the binding of the book. But each bound book must be capable of use. New books can be sewn or books that have only the pages can be resewn and provided with new covers.

You can be employed full- or part-time by colleges or firms or be self-employed. Most craft bookbinders are self-employed and bind books for individuals. You might also be asked to make expensive books for specific purposes or bind a small collection of books for a publisher. A common source of income is in binding dissertations and theses for colleges and universities and doing binding work for libraries. When repairing old books you need to match the originals in style and materials as closely as possible.

You need a sense of proportion and a good eye for design and colour. You also need to understand leather and the other materials used. You might be asked to repair antique leather items.

You would not necessarily spend all day at your bench. You could visit customers in their homes or be out and about choosing materials.

● **How many bookbinders are there?** There are about 2000 professional bookbinders in the UK.

• Job prospects and pay If you are in stable employment as a bookbinder you can earn between £200-£400 per week.

• Start-up costs Start-up costs including bookbinding press, table and tools can cost as much as £5000. You will also need the cost of renting a work shed unless you have suitable space at home.

• How old must you be? There are no age restrictions for bookbinding and you can still be working at 60 or over.

• Training There are many introductory weekend or evening courses at local colleges. You can learn the basics on a full- or part-time course. If you are lucky you might be able to get an apprenticeship with a practising bookbinder, but this is rare. Some colleges now provide courses in bookbinding and related subjects such as conservation, calligraphy and book arts. To get work as a bookbinder you need to have two to three years practical experience or an HND in binding. BTEC courses are available and Roehampton Institute offers a BA in Calligraphy or Bookbinding. For BTEC Higher National or BA courses you need A levels or the equivalent.

• Qualifications Preferably your qualifications should include three to four years training for an HND or HNC.

Contacts: *The Society of Bookbinders*, Lower Hammonds Farm, Ripley Lane, West Horsley, Surrey KT24 6JP. Tel: 01483-283175. Fax: 01483-281141. Website: **www.antiquesworld.co.uk/Tradass/bookbind.html**; *The Crafts Council*, 44a Pentonville Road, Islington, London N1 9BY. Tel: 020-7278 7700. Website: **www.craftscouncil.org.uk/home.htm**; *Roehampton Institute*, Roehampton Lane, London SW15 5PU. Tel: 020-8392 3000. Website: **www.roehampton.org.uk**

See also: Calligrapher, sculptor, saddler.
Find out about: Goldsmith.

Butler   £ £ £ £ £ +

A butler's job is to run every aspect of a large household including taking charge of the cellar and serving the wine. Although not easily placed, women can and do train as butlers. As a butler you are not simply a waiter nor a personal servant but an administrator with particular skills. In a typical day you would see to your employer's clothes, bath and breakfast, order supplies and arrange meals, shop if necessary, hire staff and be in charge of the whole running of the household. Nowadays a butler may or may not be in charge of other staff. Looking after your employer's clothing is a major part of your work and you will closely serve or supervise all meals. As you can imagine the days can be long - from 6 am to 2 am the next morning is not unusual. Although a butler can become a friend of the family it is important to draw a fine line between familiarity and work. You must be prepared to work very hard and to devote your life to the service. The perks however might include foreign travel or the satisfaction of working for celebrities.

● **How many butlers are there?** Having a butler is a private matter so no exact figures are available. But Ivor Spencer's school has trained 125 butlers. Other sources estimate that there are about 400 professional butlers working in the UK.

● **Job prospects and pay** For a properly trained butler prospects are good and salaries can start at £25,000 a year. Extras might include medical insurance, food and accommodation and the use of a car. Most butlers work for the nobility or foreign embassies, but there are considerable opportunities for work abroad.

● **Start-up costs** You will need to pay for the cost of training which at the *Ivor Butler School* is from £3500 to £3950 for a six-week course.

● **How old must you be?** You can train as a butler from 17 onwards.

● **Training** Gone are the days when you could learn on the job under the head butler in a large household. Now you need specialist training and there is only one school left in England that professionally trains butlers - *Ivor Spencer International School for Butler Administrators/Personal Assistants and Estate Managers*. Unless you have been properly trained you are little more than a waiter and will not have the skills to run a household. Nor will you be employed without the school's diploma.

● **Qualifications** No qualifications are needed, but the school will decide whether you are suitable for training. You do however need to be diplomatic, tactful and discreet.

Contact: *Ivor Spencer International School for Butler Administrators/Personal Assistants and Estate Managers*, 12 Little Bornes, Dulwich, London SE21 8SE. Tel: 020-8670 5585. Fax: 020-8670 0055.

See also: Housekeeper, personal shopper.
Find out about: Bursar, waiter.

Beautiful writing is in great demand for everything from certificates to presentational scrolls, from cards to calligraphic pictures, from hand-written books to bookplates. If you can master the craft of writing a script that is beautiful to look at and is well-designed on the page you can earn a living at it.

You might not spend your days producing a full-length book on the scale of the medieval illustrated volumes, but you might be asked to design a personalised Christmas card or design lettering suitable for wood carving.

Although it is possible to use traditional quill pens, nowadays the pens are steel-tipped and inks come in a variety of types and colours. You can use gold leaf and include coloured pen and ink pictures or designs. The art is not in just producing writing, but setting the design on the page so that the whole is a work of art.

There is a huge variety of work. You could be working in areas such as advertising, film and book titles, certificates or heraldry. You could, like many calligraphers, teach in adult education or on workshops to supplement your income. Most calligraphers are self-employed and there are opportunities for full- or part-time work.

● **How many calligraphers are there?** Because so many callig-raphers are self-employed and few belong to a recognised organisation, no numbers can be given. However, there are many thousands of people who practise calligraphy as a hobby and *The Society of Scribes and Illuminators* has 890 Lay Members as well as 72 Fellows of professional standard.

● **Job prospects and pay** The pay is what you can charge for your work. Look around and see what other calligraphers charge and pitch your rate at mid-level to start with. You will need to cover your costs. If you get to be well known as a calligrapher your work could be almost full-time.

● **Start-up costs** These can be as much or as little as you wish, but will include paper, pens, ink and reference books. You might include gold leaf later. Your costs would be a few hundred pounds for basic equipment plus a computer and perhaps Internet charges as well as somewhere to work.

● **How old must you be?** Anyone of any age can learn calligraphy and you can continue as long as you have a steady hand and good eyesight.

29

• **Training** You can teach yourself calligraphy from books, but you will learn more quickly and accurately if you attend classes. Some art training helps. Adult education classes will get you started. If you want to take it further there are BA courses in Calligraphy and Bookbinding and HND courses in Lettering as well as correspondence courses and the Advanced Training Scheme run by *The Society of Scribes and Illuminators*. Some people become calligraphers after studying it at art school and often combine it with other work such as wood and stone carving.

• **Qualifications** You don't need any qualifications although if you can show a certificate from a college course this will impress prospective clients. If you intend to teach you will need the relevant teaching qualifications.

Contacts: *The Society of Scribes and Illuminators*, 6 Queen Square, London WC1 3AR. E-mail: scribe@calligraphy.org. Website: **www.calligraphy.org**; *The Roehampton Institute*, Roehampton Lane, London SW15 5PU. Tel: 020-8392 3000. Website: **www.roehampton.org.uk**

See also: Graphologist, wallpaper designer, bookbinder, typographer, stonemason. **Find out about:** Illustrator, artist.

Cartographer (map maker) 　　　£ £ £ – £ £ £ £

If maps fascinate you and you like the idea of creating them why not think about a career in map-making (cartography). But dismiss thoughts of intrepid explorers hacking through unknown jungles to chart new territories. The job nowadays is largely office based and IT driven. A knowledge of statistics will be more useful to you as a map-maker than skill with a machete.

A modern cartographer creates maps and charts through planning, design and editing. The maps you make might be printed, but most maps and charts nowadays are digital. Much of the work is done on a computer screen using GIS (Geographical Information Systems) to scan, process and display the data. You are less likely to be involved with drawing maps than collecting the necessary data which could involve surveying, aerial photography or social and economic research. You then check the printout of the finished map for accuracy, location of features and inclusion of all relevant information. Finally, you might be involved with the publication and distribution of all kinds of cartographic products such as maps, atlases, guides, etc.

You will mainly be office-based but might take part in fieldwork occasionally. If you get the chance, make the most of putting your practical surveying and recording skills into practise. Don't be put off by the technological aspect of cartography. You also need to be interested in art and science - both also part of the map-making process.

The work can be demanding and you need to be able to work under pressure. Patience, good organising skills and an ability to handle detail are important. You will also need personal skills to work with and supervise technical staff.

● **How many cartographers are there?** There are fewer than 3500 skilled cartographers working in the public sector. You are more likely to get work in the private sector, which employs about 10,000 cartographers.

● **Job prospects and pay** Work is generally full-time and you would normally be employed by an organisation. There are not many openings for cartographers, but you could be employed by a government department such as the Ordnance Survey, Ministry of Defence or the Meteorological Office. There are some jobs with oil companies, large civil engineering firms, map publishers, universities and the public utilities. There may also be openings abroad.

The British Cartographic Society warns that you are unlikely to make your fortune from cartography! Your rewards are mostly in the knowledge of being useful and producing something aesthetically pleasing.

● **Start-up costs** You should expect your employer to provide any equipment necessary.

● **How old must you be?** If you take a relevant degree you will start work aged over 21. However, mature applicants might find it more difficult to get accepted. It is possible, if difficult, to gain work in the profession as a school leaver and train by day release. Although you can be 16 with GCSEs, being 18 with A-levels is preferable. To take a BTEC course on day-release you must be 16+.

● **Training** You can choose from a variety of ways to get qualified. There are NVQ and SVQ courses, BTEC certificates and diploma courses, undergraduate and postgraduate degrees. If possible aim for a degree in Cartography, Topographic Science, Physical Geography or Land/Hydrographic Surveying. Some Geography or Surveying courses may contain relevant mapping options. Depending on the course content some degrees in Geology or Geophysics may be accepted.

If you are at school you might be able to obtain a post in the map production field and attend a course on day- or block-release. Further training takes place on the job after you have your degree.

● **Qualifications** Standard college and university requirements for A-levels apply for degree courses. If you are a school leaver going directly into a post you will need, for a BTEC or SCOTVEC certificate or diploma, four passes at GCSE with grades A-C, although nowadays employers increasingly prefer A-Levels. These courses are usually day-release or evening classes.

Your GCSEs or Scottish Standard Grades should include Maths and your A levels or Highers should include Geography and a Science subject. Some universities may accept Advanced GSVQ level 3.

Contacts: *British Cartographic Society, Geology and Cartography Division*, School of Construction and Earth Sciences, Oxford Brookes University, Gypsy Lane Campus, Headington, Oxford OX3 0BP. Tel: 01885 433346. Website: **www.cartography.org.uk**

See also: Explorer, naval architect.
Find out about: Landscape historian, scientist, surveyor.

Cartoonist   £ – £ £ £

Are you the next Steve Bell? Have you got an aptitude for drawing and a habit of finding the parody in any situation? If so you are probably already spending most of your time drawing cartoons. Why not make it your career?

Being a cartoonist means you observe life closely and put this observational skill to work in drawings that emphasise the funny side of life. This can range from political cartoons to simple gags, from cartoon strips to single drawings. Cartoons have a wider range than is realised and can appear in magazines, newspapers and comics or be used in supporting speakers, exhibitions, conferences and presentation material or even film, TV or IT. Cartoons are also used in merchandising, toy design and many other commercial settings.

Start by practising your craft and then send cartoons to likely publications such as your local paper, community publications and so on. As you get more successful you can try national publications. Produce your work twice the intended final size on cartridge paper or drawing board in pen and ink.

Cartooning is a precarious career so don't expect to be one of the few who draw cartoons full time. You are more likely to be self-employed and/or working part-time.

● **How many cartoonists are there?** There are possibly about 1100 professionals. Probably only a few hundred of these are full-time. *The Cartoonists' Club of Great Britain* has about 250 members, the *Cartoonists' Guild* had about 40 members and *The Comic Creators Guild* has about 150 members.

● **Job prospects and pay** Even most full-time professionals are self-employed so how well you do and how much you earn will be up to you. You need to have an understanding of how a small business works and how to approach prospective employers. The more experience you get the more you can earn because the more you can charge.

● **Start-up costs** Start-up costs will not be excessive. Assuming you have a table, telephone and light you will need to spend about £150 on paper, pencils, pens, reference material such as books and magazines and ideally a fax machine. If you can afford to spend more you can make your set up more efficient.

● **How old must you be?** There are no are restrictions, but 16+ is reasonable for starting to work in earnest. You can teach yourself cartooning from an earlier age, but you need an ability to draw. Your idea of humour is likely to change as you get older so a certain maturity is advisable.

● **Training** You can teach yourself cartooning from books or take a home study course such as offered by *The College of Cartoon Art Ltd.* Cartoonists can and do go to art school, but this is not necessary. Cartooning is not a subject on any standard curriculum in the UK although you might find a local evening course in it.

● **Qualifications** You don't need any qualifications to become a cartoonist. You are judged entirely on your work.

Contacts: *The College of Cartoon Art Ltd*, The Registrar, The Moat House, 133 Newport Road, Stafford ST16 2EZ. Tel: 01785-224232. Fax: 01530-830890. E-mail: cartoonist@cartoon.co.uk. Website: **www.cartoon.co.uk**; *The Cartoonists' Guild/Club of Great Britain*, Tel/fax: 01159-810984. Website: **www.pipemedia.net/cartoons/index.htm**; *The Comic Creators Guild*, 7 Dilke Street, London SW3 4JE. Tel: 020-8677 6737. Website: **www.thebiz.co.uk**.

Charity fund raiser   £ £ – £ £ £ £ £

A worthwhile and interesting career is raising money for a charity. Many charities, particularly the large ones, now employ people especially to raise money. As a fund raiser you would not be the person on the street rattling the tin, but negotiating with companies, arranging events and finding as many ways as possible to obtain money for the charity. The fund raiser is often the third most important person in the charity. The work is flexible enough to be full- or part-time or a job share. There are also lots of self-employed charity fund raisers. You need to be passionate about the charity you are working for - if you do not care about it why should other people donate their money? You need to be a good persuader and a go-getter who can get on with people and is good at networking.

● **How many charity fund raisers are there?** The top 100 charities probably employ about nine or ten fund raisers each and the *Institute of Charity Fund Raisers* has 3000 members. But there are many more who are self-employed and many who work for the smaller charities.

● **Job prospects and pay** If you have the right qualifications and experience you should be able to get a job. The pay varies depending on where you are working and the size of charity you are working for. Pay might therefore be from £10,000 to £30,000 a year.

● **Start-up costs** The cost of any training if necessary and the usual costs of setting up an office if you are self-employed.

● **How old must you be?** There is no age restriction to the job and many people gain experience as volunteers at school age or make it a second career.

● **Training** Although training is not essential more and more charities are asking for fund raisers with degrees. Otherwise a previous career in commercial marketing or the voluntary sector would be useful. The *Institute of Charity Fundraising Managers* is the main provider of accredited training, but there are others.

• **Qualifications** Ideally you need a degree or good further education qualifications or else a background in sales and marketing or people management.

Contacts: *Institute of Charity Fundraising Managers*, 5th floor, Market Towers, 1 Nine Elms, London SW8 3NQ; *Association of Charity Officers*; Beechwood House, Wyllyotts Close, Potters Bar, Herts EN6 2HN.

See also: Political party agent.
Find out about: Press officer, public relations officer.

Chiropractor

£ £ £ £ £

Many people experience pain from a range of conditions such as low back pain, neck and arm pain, sports injuries, headaches and arthritis. These are often caused by joints not working properly which has an adverse affect on the nervous system. Often these conditions can be best treated by adjusting the joints of the spine and limbs. Chiropractors do this with their hands and the treatment is known as manipulation or adjustment. The treatment enables the body to use its own healing powers to improve health and well-being. A chiropractor diagnoses the problem and then provides the manipulation.

If you become a chiropractor you can work with people of any age because the treatment is suitable for everyone. You use no drugs or surgical procedures. Nor do your patients have to be referred to you by a GP. However, many GPs are convinced by increasing clinical evidence that chiropractic treatment will benefit many of their patients with relevant injuries and so refer patients to chiropractors.

Besides diagnosis and treatment you will also support these with individual counselling and advice about your patients' lifestyle, work and exercise routine to help them manage their conditions and prevent the problems recurring.

• **How many chiropractors are there?** There are 800 members of the *British Chiropractic Association* and altogether about 1200 members of the four chiropractor associations.

• **Job prospects and pay** There is a growing demand for chiropractic treatment. Within five years of graduation you could earn up to £100,000 a year. You could be self-employed and work full-time or part-time.

• **Start-up costs** You will need to take into account the cost of training and the cost of premises and a waiting area as well as the cost of necessary equipment. These costs will vary according to where in the country you set up your practice.

● **How old must you be?** You will need to be 18 to attend chiropractic university courses. Chiropractors do not normally work beyond the age of 70.

● **Training** It takes at least four years to become a qualified chiropractor at *The Anglo European College of Chiropractic (AECC)* which provides an undergraduate course leading to a MSc or the *University of Glamorgan* which offers a BSc(Hons) degree. *The University of Surrey* runs a two year postgraduate MSc course. After you graduate you have to undertake a period of supervised practice after which you can apply for full registration as a chiropractor with the *General Chiropractic Council.*

● **Qualifications** The imminent formation of the *General Chiropractic Council* means that from now on all chiropractors must be registered with the Council to be able to practice legally in the UK. The Council will have the responsibility for accrediting all chiropractic courses in the UK. The *British Chiropractic Association (BCA)* is the largest chiropractic association in the UK and represents 70% of chiropractors.

Contacts: *Anglo European College of Chiropractic*, 13-15 Parkwood Road, Boscombe BH5 2DF. Tel: 01202-436200; *University of Glamorgan*, School of Applied Sciences, Pontypridd CF37 1DL. Tel: 01433-482280; *European Institute of Health and Medical Studies*, University of Surrey, Stirling House Campus, Stirling Road, Guildford GU2 5RF. Tel: 01483-302239; *British Chiropractic Association*, Blagrave House, 17 Blagrave Street, Reading, Berkshire RG1 1QB. Tel: 0118-950 5950. Fax: 0118-958 8946. E-mail: britchiro@aol.com. Website: **www.chiropractic-uk.co.uk.**

See also: Reflexologist, Tai Chi teacher.
Find out about: Osteopath, physiotherapist.

Circus performer   £ – £ £ £

There is no need to run away to join the circus. You can learn circus skills and apply for a job. Traditional circuses do employ certain specialist entertainers, but many of them have been born into the business. It is therefore difficult to get a job in a traditional circus. However, there is now a New Circus movement that employs traditional acrobats, jugglers and tightrope walkers, but does not use animals. It is more related to the performing arts than the traditional circus.

You might learn to juggle, be the person on the flying trapeze or be a clown. Many modern circus performers often combine circus skills with theatre, dance, cabaret and street theatre.

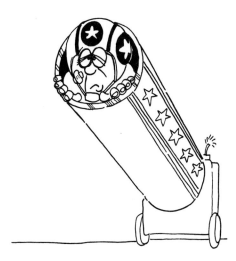

● **How many circus performers are there?** There are no figures for the number of circus performers.

● **Job prospects and pay** Your chances of being a performer in a traditional circus are small, but New Circuses sometimes have vacancies for good performers.

● **Start-up costs** You need to pay for your training.

● **How old must you be?** You can start young, but need to be old enough to be employed - normally 16.

● **Training** You might be able to teach yourself juggling skills, but acts like tightrope walking and acrobatics need specialist coaching. *Circomedia* in Bristol provides a one year foundation course in Circus skills as well as shorter courses and one day workshops.

● **Qualifications** The only qualifications you need are your skills.

Contact: *Circomedia*, Kingswood Foundation, Britannia Road, Kingswood, Bristol BS15 2DB. Tel: 0117-947 7288. Website: **www.circomedia.demon.co.uk/rabout.html**.

See also: Auctioneer, stunt artist.
Find out about: Actor, gymnast.

Classic car restorer   £ – £ £ £ £ £

Old cars still have a powerful appeal for modern drivers. Many classic cars still work and are driven proudly at classic car rallies or in annual road races. The shining body work and fact that the cars still run are testimony to the care their owners lavish on them.

Many owners of classic cars do any necessary restoring and renovating of their vehicles themselves; others prefer to leave restoring their valuable car to an expert. If you love old cars and think you can become an expert car mechanic then setting up in business as a classic car restorer might be the ideal job for you.

You will probably specialise in one particular make of car and will then need to learn everything you can about it. You need to be interested in history and have an eye for detail as well as being an expert mechanic. You also need to know where to get or how to make any missing or broken parts.

You can either work on your own account or work for a car museum or similar institution.

● **How many classic car restorers are there?** It is difficult to estimate the number because some owners restore their own cars.

● **Job prospects and pay** This is a specialised career with a limited clientele so your prospects will depend on how quickly you build a reputation for expertise and what your clients are prepared to pay.

● **Start-up costs** To set up on your own you will need the cost of premises and equipment as well as spare parts and bodies.

● **How old must you be?** You can start working on cars on private property at any age, but to set up on your own you would normally be 18+ and have a driver's license.

● **Training** Get a thorough training in car mechanics and study the history of classic cars, particularly the make in which you want to specialise. If possible, get work experience with an experienced restorer. At the very least you need practical work experience working as a garage mechanic. If you can afford it you can work on a car at home. Visit car museums, classic car rallies, talk to owners, build up contacts.

● **Qualifications** There are no specific qualifications needed except training in car mechanics and there are many NVQ courses which can satisfy this.

Contacts: Get to know owners and join the relevant classic car organisation. Advertise your services by word of mouth and in classic car magazines. *Association of Classic Car Clubs* (ACC), c/o MG Owners Club, Freepost, Swavesey, Cambridge CB4 5QZ. Tel: 01954-231125. Fax: 01954-232106; *Society of Automotive Historians* (UK Chapter) (SAH), Glaspant Manor, Capel Ifan, Newcastle Emlyn, Carmarthenshire SA38 9LS. Tel: 01559-370928. Fax: 01559-371253. Website: **www.geocities.com/motorcity/sah.html.**

See also: Blacksmith, racing driver.
Find out about: Garage mechanic, engineer, museum worker.

Colour analyst/image consultant £–£££££

This is a wonderful career if you love clothes and relish the idea of making people look their best. As a colour analyst or image consultant you work with individuals either on their own or in small groups. You help them find their best colours and the kind of clothes that will suit them best. The system works on the premise that everyone has a set of colours that suit them best and make them look younger and more healthy. Sometimes these are divided into 'seasons' so you might advise someone that they are a 'Winter' person with a particular range of colours that suit all 'Winter' people. You don't promote any particular line of clothes, but guide your clients so that they feel confident about choosing clothes and colours that suit them best. However, you might be expected to promote the company's make-up products which you will be able to buy at a discount. You might provide any or all of the following - colour analysis, make-up lessons and prescriptions, style classes, fashion updates, makeovers, bridal consultations, wardrobe weeding, personal shopping, choosing seasonal essentials, or personal image consultations for men.

Although there is no reason why men cannot be colour analysts or image consultants they do tend to be women. However, clients include both men and women. In fact your work could include providing workshops for organisations that wish to help their work force improve their image.

Most colour analyst/image consultant jobs are run on a franchise basis. That means that for a fee the parent company will train you and support you, but you have the autonomy of running your own business. The major image constancy in the UK is *Colour Me Beautiful.*

You need to be inspirational, approachable and committed.

• How many colour analysts/image consultants are there

There are several companies that train colour analysts, but *Colour Me Beautiful (CMB)* has about 170 consultants throughout the UK.

• Job prospects and pay You will be self-employed so the prospects are what you make of them. Profits range from £8-12 per person for giving a fashion update session to £50 for a full style consultation. If you are asked to help with personal shopping the fee charged is up to you.

• Start-up costs The basic kit is provided within the fee for your training session. Thereafter you can buy make-up from the company at a discount.

• How old must you be? There are no specified age limits, but many consultants are second-jobbers and the need to deal with adults and have a good level of education means that most people will be over 18.

• Training CMB modular training takes place in stages so you can build your business at your own pace and pay back the investment at minimal risk. This costs £500. For an intensive initial training course the cost is £1000-£2200. Further courses that train you in men's image, style, corporate or retail cost from £400 to £900 plus VAT.

• Qualifications There is nothing to stop you from setting up as a colour analyst or image consultant without any qualifications at all. However, the backing of a major company will give your clients more confidence. With *CMB* your title, such as colour consultant, image consultant or corporate consultant is achieved after completing the respective courses or by making a certain number of cosmetics sales.

Contacts: *Colour Me Beautiful*, FREEPOST, London SW8 3NS. Tel: 0845-603 3408. Fax: 020-7627 5680.

See also: Personal shopper, wardrobe master/mistress.
Find out about: Make-up artist.

Comedian   £ – £ £ £ £ £

So your friends fall around at your jokes and your work mates think your impersonation of the prime minister is a scream. But have you got what it takes to stand up in front of an audience for half an hour or more and make them laugh?

Being a comedian is hard work and the myth of the sad comedian is often true. It can be depressing to stand up on a stage night after night and fail to get the laughter you expect.

Your venues might be pubs, night-clubs, radio or TV (if you're lucky), holiday centres, in fact anywhere where laughter is wanted.

You can start as an amateur and practise by getting part-time work at evenings and weekends. If you become successful you'll need an agent to handle bookings and fees.

You need to be confident and thick-skinned. Most comedians have had their share of audiences who have not appreciated their sense of humour.

A comedian's life is stressful and uncertain. It is no surprise that so many comedians are tragic figures in real life. The entertainment scene is full of people out to make a fast buck and who have no hesitation in using your inexperience to do so. So you need to be alert and wary. You also need to be able to put up with unsociable working hours and hostile audiences.

- **How many comedians are there?** Everyone's a comedian.

- **Job prospects and pay** Both are uncertain, but you can make a lot of money if you hit the big time. It is rare for most comedians to get regular work. *Equity* pay for working in provincial theatre is £212.50 per week plus an allowance for lodgings.

- **Start-up costs** None.

- **How old must you be?** To work in pubs and clubs you need to be 18+.

- **Training** Watch and listen to other comedians and practise.

- **Qualifications** None.

Contacts: *Equity* (*British Actor's Equity Association*), Guild House, Upper St Martins Lane, London WC2H 9EG. Tel: 020-7379 6000. Fax: 020-7379 7001.
E-mail: info@equity.org.uk. Website: **www.equity.org.uk.**

See also: Auctioneer, circus performer.
Find out about: Actor, cartoonist.

Computer games designer   £ £ £ – £ £ £ £ £

If you are one of those people who spend all day playing computer games and actually understands how to program, then you could turn your obsession into a paying job. There is an insatiable appetite among the general public for computer games of all types from the simple puzzles to games with complex computer graphics such as *Lara Croft*. If you think you can design a better game you could make your fortune!

It takes about 20 people to produce a complex game and 187 to publish and market it. But it is possible to go it alone. It just means that you will have to provide the extras such as art work, music and publicity.

The minimum you need to design computer games is a knowledge of a modern programming language. It doesn't matter which language you use as long as you know how to use it. You can supplement your skills with useful software such as a commercial graphics library, a compiler program, and a paint program. Apart from the usual fast computer, modem and online communication you are ready to go.

You can work for yourself and sell the game to a company or you can be employed by a company to design games. Start by offering your games through shareware. This means offering a taster of your games for a specified period for people to try by buying a copy by post or downloading from your website. Hopefully they'll like the game so much that they'll pay you for the full version or the handbook - whatever the extra is that you are offering.

Look at other commercial games to find the names of potential commercial buyers. When you offer your work to anyone make sure that it has your copyright notice on it.

• How many computer games designers are there?
Practically everyone who knows how to use a computer language has tried creating their own games. So potentially thousands.

• Job prospects and pay You can earn a fortune if you are successful enough to start your own games business. Otherwise it depends on how good your games are and how effective your sales techniques are. If you are employed by a company your salary will depend on the company's own policy and your experience and qualifications. As a guide in a similar area a graduate trainee junior programmer earns from £12,000+.

• Start-up costs You need a fast computer, a modem and online communication.

• How old must you be? Teenagers have made their fortunes with good computer games compiled from their bedrooms - so you can be any age as long as the product is commercially viable.

• Training You can teach yourself a computer language from books and get started. Or you can take a university course in computers. Obviously you will have a better chance getting a job with a commercial company if you have some traditional training. Employers set their own entry requirements.

- **Qualifications** You don't need any to go it alone, but you can learn computing at university.

Contacts: Look on commercial games packets to find the names of possible sponsors. *Association of Computer Professionals*, 204 Barnett Wood Lane, Ashtead, Surrey KT21 2DB. Tel: 01372-272442; *British Computer Society*, 1 Sanford Street, Swindon, Wiltshire SN1 1HJ. Tel: 01793-417417; *Institution of Analysts and Programmers*, Charles House, 36 Culmington Road, London W13 9NH. Tel: 020-8567 2118.

See also: Wallpaper designer, web page designer.
Find out about: Computer programmer.

Cordon Bleu cook   £ £ – £ £ £ £ £

Strictly speaking in the UK you are only a *Cordon Bleu* Cook if you have trained at one of the *Cordon Bleu* schools. The UK school is in London (others are in Paris, Tokyo, Sydney, Ottawa and New York). The name derives from an ancient order of French knights who were famous for their feasts. They wore religious medallions strung from a blue ribbon around their necks (the 'cordon bleu'). This gave the cooks their name. In the late 19th century Marthe Distel started the first Le *Cordon Bleu* school in Paris and the name, now a trademark, is associated with fine cooking.

Cordon Bleu cooking is not just for upper class people or those serving food at corporate functions. Anyone with a desire to cook well can learn to become a *Cordon Bleu* cook. Students range from young people taking a Gap year course so that they can earn money cooking in ski chalets and those who want to work in restaurant kitchens. Others go into hotel or restaurant management or into food related careers such as food writing, photography or journalism.

- **How many Cordon Bleu cooks are there?** Many people call themselves cordon bleu cooks if they have learnt from books or at courses where 'cordon bleu' is used as a general description of cookery type. However, the school trains hundreds of students each year and those who complete the training satisfactorily can call themselves *Cordon Bleu* cooks or chefs.

- **Job prospects and pay** If you train at the school your job prospects are good because employers recognise the quality of *Cordon Bleu* training. Those who attend full time courses can go into the kitchens of fine restaurants to start their cookery career. Students going into industry can often expect to progress faster than those with other types of cookery training.

If you attend part-time classes or train in 'cordon bleu' type cookery elsewhere, then you can take the same career routes but will not have the backing of the school to help you. *Cordon Bleu* cooks who start out in private catering can often move into mainstream cookery if they do well.

As a guide to basic pay traditional commis chefs (trainee chefs) in a kitchen will earn about £7-8000 while head chefs can earn from £16,500-£37,500 depending on the establishment.

● **Start-up costs** The cost of training depends on the length and type of course. At the London school short classes from an evening to several days cost from £20 to £1,460 pounds. Demonstration sessions are open to the public for a fee of £15 in advance. Full time sources lasting from four to 10 weeks cost from £250 to £3,380. There are discounts for multiple enrolments and students over 30 might be eligible for vocational training relief. (For information contact the admissions office). In addition those attending full time must purchase the school's uniform and tools which could cost approximately £520.

The cost of training in other schools and at evening classes varies according to the type of course, its length and the nature of the teaching body.

The costs of starting work after the course will depend on what area of cookery you want to go into.

● **How old must you be?** Although there is no official age limit for training most are 18 or over.

● **Training** The school offers courses at many different levels and to suit both prospective professionals and those studying for pleasure only. All students are continually assessed and graded. The training is based on practical classes or workshops and demonstrations.

● **Qualifications** No previous training or experience is needed as all students start from the basics and progress through the course.

Contacts: *Le Cordon Bleu London Culinary Arts Institute*, 114 Marylebone Lane, London W1M 6HH. Freephone: 0800-980 3503 (UK only) or tel: 020-7935 3503. Fax: 020-7935 7621. E-mail: information@cordonbleu.co.uk. Website: **www.cordonbleu.net.**

See also: Vegetarian caterer, sandwich maker and seller.
Find out about: Restaurent owner, cake maker

Courier

As a courier or despatch rider you will never be replaced because there will always be a need for point to point same-day deliveries. You will take a letter or package for a customer and deliver it the same day either by motor bike or van. Usually deliveries will be in the same geographical area such as a large city like London or Manchester. But sometimes the ride will involve travelling the length of the country. Usually you will only have one package to deliver to one place, but occasionally your might have to collect several packages and make a multi-point drop.

It is rare to get real excitement such as rushing a heart to a hospital and sometimes the job can be downright boring. Try telling a courier trapped in traffic on the M1 that their life is exciting!

Couriers can be self-employed or employed by a local despatch company. Most same-day couriers in London are self-employed. Most couriers outside London are likely to be employed.

● Job prospects and pay There will always be a need for couriers so as long as you can do the job you are unlikely to be out of work. Gross pay can be £500 per week. Pay is about 20 per cent higher in London.

● Start-up costs If you are self-employed then you need to buy your motorbike or van. Fuel will cost you about £100 a week and you need to take into account the running costs of your vehicle.

● How old must you be ? You need to be old enough to hold a driving license, but insurance for very young drivers is expensive so that is usually a limiting factor in getting employment at a young age.

● Training There is not much training available although organisations provide some. The main training you need is gaining knowledge of your geographical area. The better you get to know your geographical area the more work you will be given. You can work towards NVQ level 2 in Transporting Goods by road if you wish.

● Qualifications Despatch companies do not care about qualifications, but they do want you to have a clean driving license.

Contacts: Look for jobs in the local papers, job centres and careers centres or approach despatch companies directly.

See also: Racing driver.
Find out about: Postal worker.

45

Crossword compiler

Putting your wits against someone else's ingenuity and cunning is part of the fun of doing crossword puzzles. To the average person it seems as if the people who actually compile crosswords are masters and mistresses of a highly complex art. But if you enjoy solving crosswords and enjoy playing around with words (and have a good dictionary!) you can teach yourself to compile crosswords and earn a living from it.

There are two kinds of crosswords. The first has clues that are simply straightforward definitions. The second kind has creative cryptic clues where the solver has to work out the answer from clues in a sentence. Both types of crossword can earn you money.

Start by practising solving all kinds of crosswords until you are proficient. Then use blank crosswords as a base and practise filling in your own words - not as easy at it sounds. Once you have managed to fill a few grids in, try giving them clues as one word definitions. Use a dictionary to check. Then try to play with words to make cryptic clues - read *How to Compile and Sell Crosswords and Other Puzzles* by Graham R Stevenson and *Chambers Crossword Manual* by Don Manley to learn how to compile crosswords and set them out for an editor.

Once you can do this try some on your friends and then try sending them to editors of likely magazines and newspapers. Start with local media - look for papers and magazines with no crosswords. Themed crosswords are often popular with readers so if you are sending a crossword to a farming magazine try to make the answers relate to the magazine's contents. Or if Easter is coming up use that as a theme. Try compiling other puzzles such as word searches too. For regular work try selling your crosswords to crossword magazines and puzzle books.

● **How many crossword compilers are there?** There are a dozen or more well known ones, but many more who either prefer to remain anonymous or who compile crosswords for lesser known magazines and newspapers.

● **Job prospects and pay** Once you start to sell your work you need to get a reputation for accuracy and reliability. Editors will then start to approach you. You can then also advertise in journalist magazines and other media. Your pay will be as much as you can get. You can earn as little as £10 per crossword or as much as £70 or more depending on your skill, the type of crossword and how well you are known.

● **Start-up costs** There are virtually no start-up costs except paper, pen and stamps. You can buy computer programs to help you make the grids, but these vary in reliability and ease of use.

- **How old must you be?** Any age at all as long as you can compile crosswords.

- **Training** Obviously if you know a crossword compiler then the best way to learn is to get them to talk you through the process and look at your early attempts. Otherwise teach yourself by solving crosswords and reading the books mentioned above.

- **Qualifications** None.

Contacts: Put 'crossword' into your favourite Internet search engine for crossword sites all over the world.

Croupier   £ £ – £ £ £ £   47

If you think being a croupier is all glamour and meeting the famous then you've been watching too many James Bond movies. Although a croupier is part of the entertainment business it is hard work. Croupiers deal in games of chance such as American Roulette, Blackjack and Casino Stud Poker. You work at the gaming tables of clubs and casinos and are in charge of accepting bets, allocating chips, spinning roulette wheels, dealing cards, and dealing with the money for winners and losers.

You need to be prepared to work long and unsociable hours and working most weekends. Your days off are allocated by the manager. Casinos stay open 365 days a year and typical hours are from 2pm to 4am in two shifts (1.30pm to 9pm and 9pm to 5am). As a trained croupier you could travel if you wished by working abroad or on ocean liners or even ferries. But you are likely to start by working in a provincial casino in the UK.

- **How many croupiers are there?** There are about 100+ casinos in the UK employing about 4000 people.

- **Job prospects and pay** For a trained and experienced croupier job prospects are good with the opportunity to work anywhere in the world. Once you are trained you can expect to earn £400+ per week. Your starting salary in the UK will be about £10,000 depending on where you work.

- **Start-up costs** None.

- **How old must you be?** Definitely at least 18 and preferably under 35.

- **Training** Most major gaming clubs have their own training schools. Private courses are also available. For example, *Marx Croupier Training* which for £650 will train you as a croupier over two months.

- **Qualifications** You must be scrupulously honest. You also need to be polite, of smart appearance and well groomed, cheerful under all circumstances, good at relating to the public and willing to be guided by people who may be younger than you. You should also be prepared to work shifts and antisocial hours. You need a good head for figures so GCSE maths is an advantage.

Contacts: Ask at your local job centre or contact the major gambling groups. *British Casino Association*, 29 Castle Street, Reading, Berkshire RG1 7SL. Tel: 01734-589 191. Fax: 01734-590 592. Fax: 0118-959 0592. **Website: www.british-casinos.co.uk/**; *Marx Croupier Training*, Website: **www.schatje.demon.co.uk/mct.html.**

See also: Private detective, bailiff.
Find out about: Bouncer, bank employee.

Deep sea diver £ £ £ £ £

Deep sea divers in the UK usually work on the north sea and are saturation divers. That means that they have to spend two days or longer in a compression chamber getting a mixture of oxygen and helium saturated into their bodies so that they can stay under water longer, usually up to 4 or 5 hours. Nowadays there are also armoured suits in which divers can stay under water indefinitely. A lot of deep sea diving work takes place around the oil rigs where divers are used to inspect the rigs for cracks and for future construction work. About 800 divers work on the North Sea. Divers can get work around the world and in Brazil, for example, might be working up to 300 metres under water.

Divers are often nicknamed 'underwater navvies' because you are doing manual work underwater, often in the pitch dark. You should be prepared to do non-diving work too and make yourself useful when not diving.

Although deep sea or saturation diving requires extra training, most work nowadays is in shallower water or inland. Sometimes this is as little as 20-30 feet deep. Divers who work in shallow waters use air diving techniques, that is they dive breathing compressed air from cylinders on their backs or through hoses reaching to the surface. About 1200 or so divers work in shallower waters or inland.

Most divers are self-employed for tax and national insurance purposes only. Most would like to work full-time, but there is a shortage of work so many have to work part-time.

● **How many deep sea divers are there?** There are probably about 3000 commercially qualified British divers working at any one time.

● **Job prospects and pay** There is a standard rate of pay for divers in the North Sea and this ranges from £30,000 to £100,000+ if they work there for over half the year. If you become an onshore or overseas diver and work for most of the year you can expect to earn £20,000-£35,000.

● **Start-up costs** One of the main costs is the training. A basic training course to enable you to work on the North sea as an air diver will cost about £8000. To become a saturation diver costs a further £9000. If you want to advance your career after that there are other courses to pay for. You will need your own diving suit which will cost about £300-£400. You will need to pay for a yearly medical without which you can't dive. This costs from £80-£100.

● **How old must you be?** There are no age restrictions for training or working. You would probably be foolish to train over the age of 30 although this is not impossible. The average age of North Sea saturation divers is about 41. You must be 18 before you can become a diver and you should ideally complete your training before you are 25. This is because most divers expect to leave the profession by their mid-forties.

● **Training** The basic diving course mentioned above is a must - otherwise it depends on how much you want to advance your career and what kind of diving you want to do. Details of diving qualifications are laid down by the *Health and Safety Executive (HSE)* who also supply details of the necessary courses. The Services and the police train their own divers for particular kinds of work.

- **Qualifications** All divers must have an HSE certificate of diver competence. All commercial divers must complete the basic and saturation diver courses. Again details can be obtained from the HSE. All saturation divers, including deep sea divers, must be qualified in air diving and have a minimum of one year's experience of diving up to 50 metres and have a current 'fitness to dive certificate' from an HSE approved doctor.

Contact: Michael Cocks, *Professional Divers Association*, Flat 2, 32 Kensington Park Gardens, London W11 2QS. Tel: 020-77278280; *Health and Safety Executive* (HSE), Diving Policy Section, Fourth Floor, South Side, Rose Court, 2 Southwark Bridge Road, London SE1 9HS. Tel: 020-7717 6000. Fax: 020-7717 6717. Website: **www.open.gov.uk/hse/hsehome.htm**; *The British Sub-Aqua Club*, Telford's Quay, Ellesmere Port, South Wirral, Cheshire L65 4FY. Tel: 0151-357 1951. Fax: 0151-357 1250. Website: **www.ukdiving.co.uk/ukdiving/bsac/index.html**.

See also: Hot air balloonist, racing driver, explorer.
Find out about: Marine biologist, oil rig worker, sea captain.

Dog breeder   £ – £ £ £

If you love dogs and are prepared to put in the time and money needed to breed them responsibly then you might consider becoming a dog breeder. You would not, of course, want to be one of the morally repugnant 'puppy farmers' so you will need to be committed and caring.

To start as a responsible dog breeder you will need to decide why you want to breed dogs. Just liking dogs is not enough. You must be prepared to be committed to their welfare. Next you choose the breed you are going to be interested in. Before you make a decision go to dog shows which are held all over the country. Also go to one or more of the biannual *Kennel Club* events called 'Discover Dogs'. At these events breeding clubs provide a booth so that visitors can get to know what different breeds are like and to learn about their problems and needs. Talk to responsible breeders too. Once you have made a choice, buy a bitch of the appropriate breed from a responsible dealer.

Dog breeding is time consuming and expensive. Once you have your bitch you must wait while she matures. If the breed is prone to hereditary diseases you must wait until she is old enough to be tested for the disease. If she is clear you can breed from her by paying for the services of a stud dog from a reliable breeder. If she tests positive then you have to buy a new bitch and start again.

As a responsible breeder you would not breed from a bitch every time she came into season, nor from one too young. Once your animals were old enough to sell you would need to take into account the suitability of prospective owners. Responsible breeders turn down many applicants because they cannot trust them to care for the dog.

Your first step if considering breeding dogs seriously is to contact the *British Dog Breeders Council.*

● **How many dog breeders are there?** Although there are many people who might breed one litter, and a number of irresponsible 'puppy farmers', there are only very few people who can call themselves professional dog breeders.

● **Job prospects and pay** Most breeders combine breeding with other related paying work such as running a pet shop or providing dog training. You could also get work in breeding kennels. Even as a full-time breeder your profits are likely to be small. Any money from breeding is made from selling animals rather than shows, although winning a show is good advertising.

● **Start-up costs** The accommodation you need for your dogs will vary depending on the breed you choose. A good bitch will cost from about £500 depending on the breed, and training will cost from £200. You will then need the cost of vets fees, food, dog pedigrees, Kennel club registration, etc.

● **How old must you be?** There are no rules governing the age of dog breeders. Many young people make excellent and caring handlers and learn about dogs by showing them.

● **Training** As you will be looking after living creatures it is particularly important that you take a training course. Some kennels run a course and the *British Dog Breeders Council* runs seminars. You can find details of relevant courses in *Dog World* or *Our Dog* magazines.

● **Qualifications** There are no qualifications needed at present although a law is going through parliament that will help to restrict unreliable breeders.

Contacts: Jill Terry, Secretary, *British Dog Breeders Council*, E-mail: babrees@ compuserve.com; *The Kennel Club*, 1-5 Clarges Street, Piccadilly, London W1Y 8AB. Tel: 020-7629 5828. E-mail: info@the-kennel-club.org.uk. Website: **www.the-kennel-club.org.uk**.

See also: Gamekeeper, zoo worker, shepherd, fish farmer, mobility instructor (guide dogs).
Find out about: Vet, police dog handler.

Dry stone waller   £ £ £ – £ £ £ £

Most of the dry stone field walls you can see in Britain were built from 1500-1900. Those around small fields and often twining around homesteads are the oldest. Long walls stretching over the hills are the most recent and were built during the Enclosure Acts of the 1800s. It is estimated that there are about 70,000 miles (112,000 km) of dry stone walls from the Isle of Wight to the Shetlands. The walls are made of separate pieces of stone that are fitted together without mortar. A well built stone wall will last for about 150 years; a badly built one lasts less than five. They need to be repaired and kept in good order. The type of stone used depends on the local stone available.

Besides the most common free-standing walls other uses for dry stone walling include load bearing retaining walls and domestic structures such as houses, barns and ancient monuments. A good dry stone waller works to specifications and good practice and it is an art as much as a craft.

You will need to be physically fit because there is a ton to a ton and a half of stone in each yard of a four and a half foot high wall. In an average day one person can build a 12 foot (3.6m) wall and that will mean shifting about six tons of stone!

Although it has been a dying craft there is now an upsurge of interest in dry stone walling as part of our built landscape heritage.

● **How many dry stone wallers are there?** There are about 200 professional dry stone wallers registered in the UK.

● **Job prospects and pay** Ninety-five per cent of dry stone walls are in need of restoration so your skills are needed! Typical payment for building a yard of wall is between £20-25.

● **Start-up costs** The cost of training. Weekend courses with regional branches of the *Dry Stone Walling Society* cost between £20-30 for non-members.

● **How old must you be?** There are no age restrictions.

● **Training** The *Dry Stone Walling Association of Great Britain (DSWA)* provides training courses and there are short courses available from organisations such as the *National Trust*. The craft is learnt by watching and assisting experienced wallers and by getting lots of practice.

● **Qualifications** None are needed, but the *Dry Stone Walling Association of Great Britain* has a certification scheme at four levels of competence.

Contacts: For further information about the craft, Association, courses open to the public, details of certified dry stone wallers, mail order books, etc, send a SAE to *DSWA*, c/o YFC Centre, NAC, Stoneleigh Park, Warwickshire CV8 2LG; *The National Trust*, 36 Queen Anne's Gate, London SW1H 9AS. Tel: 020-7222 9251.

See also: Stone mason, shepherd, thatcher.
Find out about: Builder, farmer, architect.

Ecologist   £ £ £ – £ £ £ £ £

Ecologists do many different jobs, so you must decide what kind of ecologist you want to be. Ecologists can be employed by the government and by statutory sector organisations such as English Nature, consultancies, and non-government organisations. The work can involve being a warden, area officer, researcher, scientist, providing field surveys and advice or international work at conferences and specialist meetings. People with volunteer experience are preferred and although degrees are necessary for science based jobs, certificates and diplomas are often acceptable. Increasingly ecologists are finding work in the media either writing, producing programmes or providing PR and campaigning expertise. Teaching at all levels also attracts ecologists.

Business and industry increasingly employ ecologists at the planning stage of construction to ensure that environmental issues are taken into account and in land and water restoration and use, maintaining and monitoring standard, horticulture and ecotourism. To be a good ecologist you need to be fascinated by animals and plants, have a thorough knowledge of how natural systems work, have good academic qualifications in biological or environmental subjects, expertise in one or more groups of living organisms, be able to make others enthusiastic about the natural world, enjoy fieldwork, be prepared to do the sometimes boring or uncomfortable tasks in the field or laboratory and have an objective approach to conservation issues. You also need to be good at teamwork, self-motivated and have good computer literacy, communication and negotiation skills.

● **How many ecologists are there?** Ecologists are found in so many different areas of life that it is impossible to say how many there are.

● **Job prospects and pay** Your job prospects will depend on which branch of ecology you want employment in and at what level you enter. In many cases your job chances will be better if you have demonstrated your commitment by volunteer work with a relevant organisation or group. If you are a student take advantage of the student membership schemes of the *British Ecological Society (BES)* or the *Institute of Ecology and Environmental Management (IEEM)*. Pay varies depending on the type of employment you achieve.

● **Start-up costs** This is not usually applicable.

● **How old must you be?** Volunteers can be any age. But as most jobs require a degree you will need to be about 17+ to apply for courses.

● **Training** Besides volunteer work consider short courses at field centres. Learn to drive and acquire up-to-date computer skills. Some employers provide on the job training leading to non-vocational qualifications. Clerical staff will need GCSEs.

● **Qualifications** You do not usually need any qualifications to volunteer although there might be opportunities to obtain on the job vocational qualifications. Higher up the career ladder a degree in ecology or biological subjects is usually necessary. Scientific positions need graduates and managers and rangers often have degrees although there are clerical and administrative jobs available, requiring only GCSEs. You will have a better chance of getting a job if you can show your worth by having been a volunteer.

Contacts: *British Ecological Society (BES)*, 26 Blades Court, Deodar Road, Putney, London SW15 2NU. Tel: 020-8871-9797. Fax: 020-8871 9779. E-mail: general@ecology.demon.co.uk. Website: **www.demon.co.uk/bes**; *Institute of Ecology and Environmental Management (IEEM)*, 45 Southgate Street, Winchester SO23 9EH. Tel: 01962-868626. Fax: 01962-868625. E-mail: Enquiries@ieem.demon.co.uk; *Environmental Council*, 212 High Holborn, London WC1V 7VW. Tel: 020-78362626. E-mail: info@envcouncil.org.uk. Website: **www.greenchannel.com.tec**.

See also: Bird sanctuary warden, zoo worker, zoologist, gamekeeper.
Find out about: Biologist.

Embalmer   £ £ £

Embalming probably originated with the Egyptians before 4000 BC. It eventually spread to Europe where it was used from about 500 AD. Modern embalming is believed to have begun in the USA during the Civil War.

Preparing bodies for burial need not be frightening or morbid. The aim is to preserve the body so that burial can take place without haste and to prevent infection before and after burial. You need to make the body look as lifelike as possible so that relatives can look at it. The treatment involves draining the blood from a vein and injecting embalming fluid into an artery. The body's internal organs are then treated generally using one or two small incisions. The embalmed body may then have makeup applied and the hair washed and styled. The whole treatment is complicated and detailed. You need to be not only skilled and unsqueamish but also sensitive to relatives' feelings and have a respect for the dead.

You can be self-employed or work full-time. Full-time embalmers are normally employed by funeral directors.

● **How many embalmers are there?** There are 1329 members of the *British Institute of Embalmers* (BIE) and 323 students. However, some unqualified people carry out embalming.

● **Job prospects and pay** An average salary is about £15,000 a year or £15-£50 per case.

● **Start-up costs** The start-up costs include membership of the BIE which at present (1999) is £112 for three years' student membership, then £38 annually. Full member ship is £80 per year. The cost of training will depend on your tutor and whether your course is full- or part-time or by correspondence. If you want to become self-employed you will need the cost of equipment.

● **How old must you be?** There is no upper age limit and someone under 16 would probably not be considered suitable.

● **Training** Training takes place through private schools. The exam board is autonomous and the course is modular with a final exam and a practical exam. It usually takes about three years to complete training.

● **Qualifications** Your qualification would be from the National Examination Board of Embalmers followed by membership of the BIE.

Contacts: Administration Secretary, *British Institute of Embalmers*, Tel: 01564-778991. Fax: 01564-770812. E-mail: international.bie@virgin.net. Website: **www.bie.org.uk**; Secretary, NEBE, 39 Poplar Grove, Kennington, Oxford OX1 5QN, Tel: 01685 735788.

See also: Taxidermist, undertaker.
Find out about: Make-up artist, pathologist.

Embroiderer £ – £ £ £ £ £

Beautiful embroidery has always been admired and is often as much an art as a craft. If you want to excel at embroidery you need more than just skill with your hands and good eyesight. You need an understanding of different techniques and materials as well as design and colour skills.

Embroidery covers a wide range of subjects from tapestry to wall hangings, from embroidering clothing to producing works of art.

Although traditionally embroidery is done by hand you will need to understand designing through computers and the use of sewing machines.

You can make a reputation for yourself simply by practising your craft. There are many adult education courses in embroidery techniques and art and design that will help you. Enter competitions to learn how your work compares to others. You can sell your work at craft fairs or persuade shops to take it or offer your work by word of mouth.

If you want professional training then art schools have courses in textiles which can include embroidery. You could consider an organisation such as the *Royal School of Needlework*. This takes on eight apprentices who learn their craft over three years at the school. The course covers embroidery techniques, art and design, computer studies, projects and museum visits.

You can work full- or part-time. Many embroiderers are freelance.

• How many embroiderers are there?

There are about 2000 professional embroiderers in the UK and about 100,000 amateur embroiderers.

• Job prospects and pay
Embroiderers trained at the *Royal School of Needlework* have excellent prospects. For others it will depend on who employs you, or if you are self-employed, how much you can charge for your work.

• Start-up costs
The start-up costs will depend on what type of professional embroidery is taken up, but will include materials, books, etc.

• How old must you be?
There are no age restrictions. Indeed many embroiderers first learn embroidery as a child and others take it up later in life. Royal School apprentices are aged 18-26.

• Training
You can teach yourself from books or attend evening classes and courses. The Royal School apprenticeship training has been mentioned above. There are other schools which also train embroiderers.

• Qualifications
Qualifications are not needed, but Royal School graduates are awarded a Royal School of Needlework Diploma in Embroidery. Certain universities provide degree courses in embroidery.

Contacts: *Royal School of Needlework*, Apartment 112A, Hampton Court Palace, Surrey KT8 9AU. Tel: 020-8943 1432. Fax: 020-8943 4910. E-mail: rnwork@intonet.co.uk. Website: **www.royal-needlework.co.uk**.

See also: Wigmaker, wardrobe master/mistress.
Find out about: Dressmaker, tailor.

You might think there are no new parts of the world to discover. But there are vast areas of the earth where no or few people have set foot. Other areas have only been partially explored or else imperfectly recorded. The scope for exploration is still wide open - everything from jungles to the arctic, from the sea beds to the mountains or deserts. There are still adventures to be had.

However keen you are, you would be foolish to explore without having had a lot of experience of expeditions. You can get this through many organisations who arrange expeditions. Or else the *Expeditionary Advisory Centre* at The Royal Geographical Society can give you advice and help if you are organising an expedition. It also produces many useful publications for potential volunteers.

Remember that you need to be physically fit and to have had experience of the kind of terrain that you will be facing. You will need money to finance the expedition and to pay for your food and equipment and return fares. You will also need advice about visas and medication, the support of the government of the country you are going to, and appropriate support and back-up arrangements. You will probably need volunteers to go with you.

No one will go with you unless you have proved yourself trustworthy and capable. So taking part in expeditions and then working your way up to leading them is important. You can then start to lead your own expeditions to far flung places. Fiennes is probably the best known modern explorer.

● **How many explorers are there?** There are very few explorers who are genuinely breaking new ground.

● **Job prospects and pay** Unless you have a sponsor you will have to raise the money yourself and will have to work at another job until you can pay for the expedition. Unless you can earn some money by writing or making a film about your experiences when you return home you are unlikely to make a profit.

● **Start-up costs** These will be considerable and will depend on where you go and for how long. But you will need food, fares, equipment, clothing, medication, etc. The cost will be in thousands of pounds. Training courses or taking part in expeditions to gain experience can cost from £200 to £3000 or more.

● **How old must you be?** You can take part in arranged expeditions from the age of 16 or younger with various organisations, but to run your own expedition you will be unlikely to command respect until over the age of 21. Some expedition organisations such as the *Brathay Exploration Group* take young people specifically, in this case 16-25.

● **Training** Survival training and such skills as mountaineering, canoeing, etc, might be necessary, depending on the type of exploration you will be doing.

● **Qualifications** You don't need any qualifications, but you do need the practical and leadership skills that command respect among others. Remember that your own safety and that of your team will depend on you.

Contacts: *Expedition Advisory Centre*, Royal Geographical Society, 1 Kensington Palace Gore, London SW7 2AR. Tel: 020-7581 2057. Fax: 020-7581 2057 E-mail: info@rgs.org Website: **www.rgs.org/trindex.html**; *Brathay Exploration Group*, Brathay Hall, Ambleside, Cumbria LA22 0HP. Tel: 015394-33942 (expeditions and training courses for people aged 16-25); *Dorset Expeditionary Society*, c/o Budmouth Technology College, Chickerell Road, Weymouth, Dorset DT4 9SY. Tel: 01305-775599. Fax: 01305-766389 (expeditions for people aged 16-21); *Trekforce Expeditions*, 134 Buckingham Palace Road, London SW1W 9SA. Tel: 020-7824 8890. Fax: 020-7824 8892. E-mail: trekforce@dial.pipex.com. Website: **www.dialspace.dial.pipex.com/town/parade/hu15/home.htm**.

See also: Racing driver, deep sea diver, hot air balloonist, mountain guide, tour leader.
Find out about: Sailor.

Falconer   £ – £ £ £ £ £

The joy of training a falcon and watching it swoop through the air on its way to capture some prey is allied to the power it displays. Training a falcon is a long term project requiring patience, firmness and love. You need to be unafraid of such powerful birds and at the same time willing to patiently teach and learn with them. You will spend a lot of time on boring routine tasks such as cleaning out bird quarters, etc, but the rewards are an outdoor life working with intelligent creatures.

Your work might include working in a public centre and teaching falconry to the general public through lessons, hunting trips or by demonstration. There are a few jobs as a falconer looking after someone else's bird. Otherwise you can be employed to use your own falcon to clear landfill sites, airport runways, churches and town squares of pigeons. Finally falconers are often called upon to demonstrate falconry for education programmes, books and so on. So the work can be full- or part-time or you can be self-employed.

- **How many falconers are there?** About 3500 including private falconers and the few that have a career in falconry.

- **Job prospects and pay** There are few full-time jobs in falconry and most of them involve menial chores. The pay can be anything from nothing at all to £30,000 as director of a falconry centre. A lot of falconry work is seasonal and falconers are not generally well paid.

- **Start-up costs** These vary depending on how may birds you buy and whether you want to set up a falconry centre.

- **How old must you be?** There are no official restrictions although you would be unlikely to get a job under the age of 16 years.

- **Training** There is no specific training although there are courses available. There are also falconry clubs throughout the country and many of them run apprenticeship schemes for would be falconers.

- **Qualifications** None needed at present.

Contact: *British Falconers Club.* E-mail: falconers@zetnet.co.uk. Website: **www.users.zetnet.co.uk/bfc/hist.com.**

See also: Bird sanctuary warden, gamekeeper.
Find out about: Pigeon racer, budgie breeder.

Feng Shui consultant   £ £ £ £ £

Feng Shui (usually pronounced *fung shway*) is the Far Eastern practice of living in harmony with your environment. This harmony is created by using the art of placement. A house or room is divided into different areas each representing an element (such as fire or water) and an attribute (such as wealth or family). The way you arrange your space and the objects and colours you use can improve your life. At least that's the theory.

However, many people today take Feng Shui very seriously and indeed even large companies are inviting Feng Shui consultants in to ensure that both buildings and their interiors are positioned and furnished according to Feng Shui principles.

If you believe that rearranging your surroundings can affect the quality of your life and you get on well with people then earning your living as a Feng Shui consultant might appeal to you. This is a career where most practitioners are self-employed either on their own or with a partner running a consultancy. The work can be full- or part-time.

• How many Feng Shui consultants are there? There are probably about 200 Feng Shui consultants in the UK, of which about 60 are registered with the *Feng Shui Society*.

• Job prospects and pay Feng Shui is very popular at the moment. You are likely to get work through word of mouth and your reputation will grow as your experience improves. Pay varies but is usually calculated on an hourly rate. An average payment is about £250 for two hours work plus the cost of any travel involved.

• Start-up costs Start-up costs are minimal. You will need reference books and the usual costs of setting up a home office. Your main cost will be for training.

• How old must you be? There are no age limits, but most established consultants are in their 30s or 40s.

• Training There are no specific training requirements. How much you need depends on your previous experience. An architect, for example, who wanted to include Feng Shui as part of his work would probably need less training than someone learning Feng Shui from scratch. You can teach yourself from books, but reputable training will enhance your prospects. This could cost as much as £6000-£7000.

• Qualifications You don't need any qualifications, but you should join the Feng Shui Society which asks its members to sign up to a voluntary code of ethics.

Contacts: *Feng Shui Society*, 377 Edgware Road, London W2 1BT. Tel: 07050-289 200. Fax: 020-8566 0898. E-mail: karenayers@fengshuisociety.org.uk. Website: **www.fengshuisociety.org.uk**

See also: Graphologist, astrologer.
Find out about: Architect, interior designer.

Fingerprint officer   £££££ – £££££

As a police officer you have a varied and interesting choice of careers. If you have the aptitude and your Chief Constable agrees, you might have the opportunity to train as a fingerprint officer (officially called a Scene of Crime Officer, SOCO).

As a fingerprint officer you operate as part of the regional police force to which you are attached. Your job is to see that evidence present at the scene of crime or accident is preserved and your main role is collecting fingerprints and palm prints. Not only do you collect prints from objects at a scene but from people who have access to the scene or who have helped confirm someone's identity. You would also have to attend post mortems to photograph clues arising from the examination. Photography would play an important part in your work.

You need to be comfortable with learning to use new technology. You also need good manipulative skills, 100% colour vision, an eye for detail and methodical approach, have an analytical mind and be able to think laterally, be reliable under pressure, relate well to others and have good written and oral communication. You must be prepared to work to a flexible agenda, for long hours and be able to cope with distressing circumstances.

● **How many Fingerprint officers are there?** The Home Office does not keep central records for the number of fingerprint officers.

● **Job prospects and pay** Job prospects are a matter for individual forces and their Chief Constables as you would be employed by a UK Police Force. Conditions of pay and service are based on those used by local authorities. Your local force can tell you present salary levels.

● **Start-up costs** None.

● **How old must you be?** You must be at least 17. Apart from that as long a you have the right personal skills and qualities as well as emotional maturity your age does not matter. Older applicants must be able to cope with heavy lifting and carrying and working in uncomfortable surroundings. You might be asked to take a medical examination.

● **Training** Unlike other jobs within the police where training is administered at regional level, as a fingerprint officer you would be able to attend national courses at the *National Training Centre for Scientific Support to Crime Investigation* in County Durham. This Centre is a single centre of excellence, teaching best practice to Crime Scene Officers. It is administered by Durham Constabulary and is accredited by National Police Training and the University of Durham. Apart from police personnel, a few privately funded individuals suited to police work are allowed to attend. You attend courses ranging from an Initial Course for newly appointed fingerprint bureau staff to Intermediate Courses for more experienced staff and Advanced Courses when you are considered to be 'expert' status. You also get a chance to update your knowledge with refresher courses.

● **Qualifications** You must have a driving licence. The other qualifications you need will depend on which Police Force you apply to. You might need anything from GCSEs (A-C grades) or Scottish equivalents to A levels/Highers. Subjects that show good use of English and science subjects are preferred. BTEC/SCOTVEC qualifications are also accepted. You might also be considered if you have photographic qualifications and/or experience or a background/qualifications in science.

Contacts: Look for jobs in the local press and Police Review or contact your local Police Headquarters for information. Centre Support Manager, *The National Training Centre for Scientific Support to Crime Investigation*, Harperley Hall, Fir Tree, Crook, Co. Durham DL15 8DS. Tel: 01388-762191. Fax: 01325-742509. E-mail: admin@ntcss-ci.demon.co.uk.

See also: Private detective.
Find out about: Detective, pathologist, photographer.

Fish farmer   £ £ – £ £ £ £

Whether you like fish because they are good to eat or you are a keen angler, the job of a fish farmer may be the one for you. UK fish farms breed fish for either eating or sport. Some fish are raised in ponds and others are reared in sea cages in open water. There are also related jobs breeding ornamental fish and maintaining fish stocks in rivers and lakes for anglers. Most fish farms rear trout or salmon, but others breed halibut, lobster and other fish for eating. About half the fish farms are in Scotland although they are found throughout the UK.

As a fish farmer you would normally own a fish farm and employ others - farm managers, farm workers, scientists - to test for new ways of improving conditions, stocks and controlling diseases - and bailiffs - to look after the general welfare of the fish farm from start to finish. As a fish farmer you have responsibility, along with your farm mangers, for the general running of the farm and for dealing with the necessary bookkeeping, sales and transport of the fish.

It makes sense if you are starting out to gain experience by starting as a fish worker or hatcher and then becoming a fish manager or bailiff. Once you have learnt how a fish farm operates you can then apply your expertise.

Most fish farms are small and in remote places and employ only one or two people. The work is physically demanding as you work outdoors in all weathers. There is a lot of weekend and seasonal work. The spawning and harvesting times are particularly demanding and can entail being on call 24 hours a day. You need to be careful and aware, because intensive farming methods mean that disease can spread rapidly.

- **How many fish farmers are there?** There are about 500 fish farmers in the UK.

- **Job prospects and pay** If you are working your way up then your pay would be about £10,000+ as a technician, £11,000+ as a bailiff, £14-15,000+ as a scientist and £15-20,000+ as a manager. Once you are an owner your earnings would depend on the profits your fish farm makes.

- **How old must you be?** You can start as a worker/assistant at 16.

- **Training** You can be self taught and most training is on the job although there are courses available in fish farming and fish management. You should take a full-time course such as an HND if possible to get full technical training.

- **Qualifications** There are level 2 NVQs available in fish husbandry and certificates, diplomas and degree courses in fish farming and agriculture. The *Institute of Fisheries Management* offers a diploma in fisheries management if you have taken its correspondence course and passed the certificate.

There are no formal qualifications for being a fish farm worker or bailiff. Scientists naturally need a relevant degree. Generally you need to be physically fit, prepared to work outside in all weathers and able to work on your own initiative.

Contacts: *British Trout Association*, 8 Lambton Place, London W11 4PH. Tel: 020-7221 6065. Website: **www.fishlink.co.uk/trout**; *Institute of Fisheries Management*, Balmaha, Coldwells Road, Holmer, Hereford & Worcester HR1 1LH; *The Environment Agency*, 25th floor, Millbank Tower, 21-24 Millbank, London SW1P 4Xl. Tel: 020-7863 8600. Fax: 020-7863 8650; *Barony College*, Tel: 01387-860251. Fax: 01387-860397. Website: **www.ac.uk/barony-main.htm**; *Sparsholt College Hampshire*, Sparsholt, Winchester, Hampshire SO21 2NF. Tel: 01962-776441. E-mail: enquiry@sparsholt.ac.uk. Website: **www.hants.gov.uk/istcclr/cch33140.html**; *Centre for Environment, Fisheries and Aquaculture Science* (CEFAS), Pakefield Road, Lowestoft NR33 0HT. Tel: 01502-524562. Website: **www.cefas.co.uk/**.

See also: Gamekeeper, shepherd, ecologist.
Find out about: Marine biologist.

Forest officer/forest ranger

As you walk through a forest or wood remember that most forests in Britain are managed. Trees are grown for their timber. At the same time forest officers and other forest workers have to ensure that felling trees has as little harmful impact on the environment as possible. Other forests and woods are maintained as leisure facilities for the public. But even this entails necessary culling of tress, replanting and monitoring the impact on the local environment. This can mean not only ensuring that the tress are visually attractive, but that consideration is given to maintaining and encouraging the woods' wildlife.

If you become a forest officer you would start on a lower grade as a technical supervisor planning and controlling operations in the woods. Later you could move into management and plan, control and implement policies and operations operatives for more specialist work.

You can learn about forestry by starting as a forest worker doing general manual work and operating machines in the forest for a wide range of work including planting, fencing and timber harvesting.

You can work for the *Forestry Commission*, local authorities, or private individuals with large estates.

Some forest workers in the *Forestry Commission (Forest Enterprise)* may work as forest rangers. In this job you deal with wildlife and conservation. You protect wild animals and birds by creating and maintaining habitats, controlling pests and conserving the forest environment. The forest must be protected from misuse by the general public. You need to supervise and take care of public facilities such as car parks, picnic sites, etc.

● **How many forest officers are there?** *Forest Enterprise* has about 3500 staff.

• **Job prospects and pay** A trainee forest worker starts at about £90 per week at 16 rising to about £150 for a forest craftsperson. Forest officers earn about £14,000+. A forest ranger trainee can earn about £163 per week and a head ranger earns about £275 per week.

• **Start-up costs** Your employer supplies tools, machinery, etc.

• **How old must you be?** You can become a trainee forest worker at 16.

• **Training** Most training is on the job, but forest officers can take courses in forestry.

• **Qualifications** Forest workers are encouraged to take NVQs levels 1-2 and City and Guilds certificates, but these are not necessary for job applications. Forest officers can take a BTEC/SCOTVEC diploma in Forestry or study it to degree level. They can also become members of the *Institute of Chartered Foresters*. A driving licence is an advantage. All forestry employees need to be physically fit and prepared to work outside. Forest officers must be able to organise others and be prepared to do some office work.

Contacts: *The Forestry Commission*, Personnel Management Branch, 231 Corstorphine Road, Edinburgh EH12 7AT. Tel: 0131-334 0303. Website: **www.forestry.gov.uk/**; *Institute of Chartered Foresters*, 7a Colme Street, Edinburgh EH3 6AA. Tel: 0131-225 2705. Fax: 0131-2206128. E-mail: icfor@btinternet.com. Website: **www.btinternet.com/~icfor/icfweb.htm**; *The Royal Forestry Society of England, Wales and Northern Ireland*, 102 High Street, Tring, Herefordshire HP33 4AF. Website: **www.rfs.org.uk/**; *The Royal Scottish Forestry Society*, 62 Queen Street, Edinburgh EH2 4NA. Tel: 0131-2258142; Forest Enterprise, Website: **www.forestry.gov.uk/fe.html**

See also: Ecologist, gamekeeper, landscape gardener.
Find out about: Biologist, farmer.

French polisher

That wonderful shine you see on old wooden furniture is often French Polish, that is a way of treating and preparing wood to produce a smooth finish. But there is more to French polishing than just applying the final polish. You prepare the surfaces and then use stains and finishes to produce the desired effect. Other items such as panelling and doors can also be French Polished.

The aim is to prepare and treat wood to give it a smooth finish and enhance the natural quality of the wood. You can work on old and new furniture or work on fixed timber such as panelling and doors in old houses, business premises and churches. Old paint, lacquer or varnish is stripped off the wood and dents and holes filled until the surface is smooth. You might also deal with simple repairs. You then mix stains to produce the desired colour which is put on the wood with a wadded cloth known as a rubber. Then French polish is put on with another rubber covering a small area at a time until the right effect is achieved. You will also use other finishes such as varnish, lacquer, oil or wax.

You are likely to work in a small French Polishing firm employing one or two craftspeople. Otherwise you might be employed by other woodworking or cabinet making businesses, or craft or antiques restorers. Occasionally furniture manufacturers employ French Polishers to finish furniture parts that cannot be done by machine.

You need to wear safety gloves, mask and overalls while mixing and applying chemicals.

• **Job prospects and pay** There are job opportunities all over the UK. You can also be self-employed and visit clients' homes or business premises to treat furniture. There are sometimes opportunities for French polishers to rise to supervisory positions. An average minimum pay is about £181 per week.

• **Start-up costs** If you are self employed you need the cost of your equipment.

• **How old must you be?** There are no upper age limits.

• **Training** You should expect to train on the job and learn from experienced French polishers while attending college on day-release. You study for City and Guilds in, for example, Furniture Production (Polishing and Finishing). You can also get NVQs at levels 1-3. There are certificate and diploma courses in related subjects such as furniture restoration. Some private fee-paying courses are available.

• **Qualifications** There are no formal qualifications required.

Contacts: *BFM Training Ltd*, 30 Harcourt Street, London W1H 2AA. Tel: 020-7724 0851. Fax: 020-7 706 1924. Website: **www.bfm.org.uk/**; *British Antique Furniture Restorers' Association (BAFRA)*, The Old Rectory, Warmwell, Dorchester, Dorset DT2 8HQ. Tel: 01305-854822. Fax: 01305-852104. Website: **www.bafra.org.uk/**; *The Guild of Master Craftsmen (GMC)*, Castle House, 166 high street, Lewes, East Sussex BN7 1XU; *Midland School of French Polishing*, 18a Mansfield Road, Eastwood, Nottinghamshire NG16 3AQ.

See also: Antiques dealer.
Find out about: Cabinet maker.

A gamekeeper looks after the game such as pheasants or deer on his employer's estate. He or she must ensure that the birds or animals are reared safely until they are ready to be killed either by the employer or a commercial or syndicate shoot for sport. Although you would enjoy the rewards of working outdoors, you do need to be physically fit and prepared to work in all weathers. The demands of the job mean that your social life might suffer: the job continues each day until it is finished - there are no fixed hours. The best way to start is to get work experience, but not many gamekeepers have the time to show you the ropes so if you have a friend of the family who can introduce you, so much the better. Most gamekeepers are full-time, but some syndicates employ part-time self-employed gamekeepers to rear pheasants from 7-8 weeks old.

● **Job prospects and pay** There are about 3500 full-time and 2000 part-time gamekeepers, and vacancies are few and fiercely sought after. Basic pay is equivalent to a farm labourer - at present less than £200 a week - but you might get tips during the season on a commercial shoot. Most gamekeepers get a tied cottage (not always the bonus it might appear), a suitable vehicle, free use of a phone, a suit of clothes and waterproofs at least once every other year, free dog food, etc.

● **Start-up costs** None.

● **How old must you be?** There are no age restrictions. Both school leavers and mature applicants can attend college or be accepted onto shooting estates.

● **Training** You do not need any training although many estates are demanding better trained and qualified workers. There is really no substitute for practical experience under the guidance of a professional gamekeeper. However, there are many practical courses available that prepare people for a career in gamekeeping. These are either gamekeeping courses or in related areas such as management, conservation, forestry and woodland management.

● **Qualifications** You do not need qualifications, but there are one, two and three year courses that offer certificates, diplomas or NVQs in Gamekeeping. NVQs are for those already working in gamekeeping. *The British Association for Shooting and Conservation (BASC)* can provide a list of relevant colleges and courses if you send an A5 SAE. Young members of the *BASC* can take part in the Arbuthnott Award. Study is at your own pace and awards are given for units such as shotgun safety, gun dog training, and rearing game.

Contact: *The British Association for Shooting and Conservation (BASC)*, Marford Mill, Rossett, Wrexham LL12 0HL. Tel: 01244-573000. Fax: 01244-573001. E-mail: enq@basc.demon.co.uk. Website: **www.basc.org.uk**; *Easton College* Tel: 01603-742105. Fax: 01603-741438. E-mail: mail@easton-college.ac.uk. Website: **www.easton-college.ac.uk**.

See also: Bird sanctuary warden, shepherd, falconer, forest officer.
Find out about: Farmer.

Gem cutter   £ – £ £ £

Gem cutting and polishing used to be a popular hobby. However, the ability to cut and polish gemstones can also be an interesting and enjoyable career. The work involves using machines that use abrasive action to cut and polish rough gemstones so that they emerge as gems that can be used in jewellery. In fact some independent gem cutters also make simple jewellery using the gems they have created.

You do not need to know a lot about geology, but you do need to appreciate the different qualities of stones and enjoy their beauty.

The techniques used are sawing, grinding, sanding, lapping, polishing, drilling and tumbling. Sawing cuts rough stones into thin slabs; grinding shapes gemstones into a desired rough form and sanding does the same with finer abrasives; lapping is similar to grinding and sanding, but is done on one side of a stone to create flat surfaces as in facetting; polishing gives the surface a shine and brings out the inner beauty of the stone; drilling creates holes. Tumbling is a method of polishing stones into attractive random shapes over a period of many weeks. This is a popular method with beginners.

Once the gems have been cut and polished into the desired shape and size they can be further cut to produce specific types of gems such as cameos or cabochons.

You can tumble beach finds and sell them or make them into simple jewellery. Or you can buy rough gemstones and cut and polish them. You would normally buy rough stones from a reputable supplier. You can then sell them to jewellery makers or make your own jewellery. There are many basic kits available for doing that.

You need to be safety conscious because many of the machines used for cutting and polishing can be dangerous.

● **How many gem cutters are there?** There are hundreds of people who cut and polish stones for pleasure as well as for profit.

- **Job prospects and pay** Your best long term employment would be with a commercial firm. As an independent gem cutter much will depend on the cost of the gemstones and whether you have a market for the finished stones.

- **How old must you be?** Any age.

- **Start-up costs** You can start with a basic tumbler costing from £60-70. This holds about 3lb (1.36kg) of stones. Add further equipment, such as cutting machines, as and when you can afford them.

- **Training** You can be trained in particular techniques such as polishing or engraving by working in specialised companies or in departments of larger companies. If you want to be independent it would be better to learn your trade with a firm first. However, you can teach yourself from books, but obviously you will learn more quickly if you can find someone to show you the techniques.

- **Qualifications** No specific qualifications are needed.

Contacts: To learn about gems in general: *Gem Association and Gem Testing Laboratory of Great Britain*, 27 Greville Street (Saffron Hill Entrance), London EC1N 8SU. Tel: 020-7404 3334. Fax: 020-7404 8843. E-mail: gagtl@btinternet.com. Website: **www.gagtl.ac.uk/gabout.htm**. One place to buy gem cutting and polishing machine is *Evans Lapidary Machines*, 54 Beesfield Lane, Farningham, Dartford, Kent DA4 0BZ. Tel: 01322-862252. For natural crystals and gems try *Manchester Minerals*, FREEPOST (SK1439), Stockport, Cheshire SK4 1YA. Tel: 0161-477 0435. Fax: 0161-4805095 (catalogue £3).

Genealogist   £ – £ £ £

Most genealogists are part-time and self-employed although full-time professional genealogists do exist. You probably already have an interest in genealogy and have spent time tracing your own family tree. To trace any family you need to start from the known and work back towards the unknown. If you trace families for other people you first check that the information they have given you is correct and then steadily work back through the generations using birth, marriage and death certificates, parish registers and a variety of other documents to provide proof each step of the way. You would then write a written report for your client.

Record Agents search out particular documents for specific information needed by a genealogist. Some genealogists act in both capacities.

Genealogists are sometimes employed by record offices, but usually only on a part-time basis. You might be asked to trace all kinds of people - famous people, historical people, or simply an ordinary family. You might even be asked to compile an imaginary family tree for use in a book.

You need to have a good knowledge of records and where to find them as well as practice in using them effectively. You also need to be tactful and discreet - you never know what information you might turn up.

● **How many professional genealogists are there?** The *Association of Genealogists and Record Agents (AGRA)* has about 69 members.

● **Job prospects and pay** You can advertise in one of the genealogy magazines such as *Family History* or *Genealogists' Magazine*. You will usually charge by the hour and how much you earn depends on whether you work full-or part-time and how much you charge. Fees are usually calculated on an hourly basis for the time spent on research and for giving advice. You might give an initial estimate or agree a limit such a two days worth of searching beforehand. An average hourly charge is about £15-18 per hour. Genealogists employed by record offices (usually archivists) might earn about £12,000 a year.

● **Start-up costs** There are few start-up costs apart from a computer and reference books and the cost of any training you choose to undertake.

● **How old must you be?** Anyone can be a genealogist, but professional genealogists tend to be over 18.

● **Training** It is perfectly possible to teach yourself genealogy by reading books and going to evening classes. You would then put in a lot of practice before advertising your services. However, there are courses that provide a specialised training. The *Institute of Heraldic and Genealogical Studies* runs courses and a correspondence course with various levels of assessment and examinations, including an assessment as a Record Agent. The *Society of Genealogists* runs its own courses and the *Federation of Family History Societies* publishes information about courses and qualifications. You need a good general education and a broad knowledge of social and local history sources. You also need some knowledge of palaeography (old handwriting) and Latin. Your reports need to be word processed or typed so you need keyboard skills. Young people are advised to try to get training in a related field first such as archive administration, historical research, librarianship or teaching. The *Centre for Extra-Mural Studies of London University* runs a two-year certificated course in Genealogy and the History of the family which can lead to a third Diploma year.

● **Qualifications** It helps to have a qualification if you are advertising and the usual step is to become a member of the *Association of Genealogists and Record Agents (AGRA)* or get a Record Agent qualification from the *Institute of Heraldic and Genealogical Studies.* Some full-time genealogists have already qualified as a librarian or an archivist which gives them a good basis for further study.

Contacts: *Society of Genealogists,* 14 Charterhouse Buildings, Goswell Road, London EC1M 7BA. Tel: 020-7251 8799. Fax: 020-7250 1800. E-mail: Info@sog.org.uk; *Association of Genealogists and Record Agents (AGRA),* 29 Badgers Close, Horsham, West Sussex RH12 5RU; *Association of Scottish Genealogists and Record Agents,* PO Box 174, Edinburgh EH3 5QZ; *Association of Professional Genealogists in Ireland,* c/o Genealogical Office, 2 Kildare Street, Dublin 2; *Centre for Extra-Mural Studies,* 26 Russell Square, London WC1B 5DQ. Tel: 020-7631 6652; *Federation of Family History Societies,* The Administrator, The Benson Room, Birmingham and Midland Institute, Margaret Street, Birmingham BS 3BS. Website: **www.ffhs.org.uk.**

See also: Private detective, graphologist.
Find out about: Archivist, librarian, record agent.

Glass blower   £ £ £

You have probably seen glassblowers in films or on TV. They stand stripped to the waist in front of a blazing furnace while blowing through a tube to form glass tubes or shapes.

But this is not the only type of glass blower. There are three types of glass blowers: scientific, commercial and studio. So if you like the idea of working with glass you will need to decide what kind of glass blower you want to be.

If you become a scientific glass blower you normally work in a laboratory or university department. You work with silica or borosilicate tubes and use a 'lamp' to heat the glass to a workable temperature. You might also diversify by producing artistic or animal forms.

On the other hand you might prefer to work as a commercial glass blower for one of the major glass manufacturers such as Royal Doulton. You blow lead crystal into high value products.

Then there are studio glass blowers who are often art graduates or redundant craftspeople who set up on their own or as part of an artistic group. If you want to push the boundaries of glass blowing and create new designs yourself this might interest you.

Glass is not just transparent or opaque. It can be created in many colours depending on what substances are added to the raw material of sand.

Glass blowing does not just produce vessels, it can be used to make flat glass, jewellery, figurines and many other items.

● **Job prospects and pay?** A glassblower earns about £260 per week.

● **Start-up costs** You will need premises, a furnace and tools if starting on your own.

● **How old must you be?** 16+

● **Training** You will learn most by working with an experienced glass-blower. The *British Society of Scientific Glassblowers* and some London-based firms might send you to college on day-release. As a commercial glass blower you will get a lot of training before moving up to become a head blower.

Qualifications Most glass blowers have no specific qualifications, but designers usually have degrees.

Contacts: *Society of Glass Technology*, Don Valley House, Savile Street East, Sheffield S4 8UQ. Tel: 0114-263 4455. Fax: 0114 263 4411; *Glass Training Ltd*, BGMC Building, Northumberland Road, Sheffield S10 2UA. Tel: 0114-2661494/0114-2669263. Fax: 0114-2660738. E-mail: gtl@glasstrg.demon.co.uk. Website: **www.glasstrg.demon.co.uk;** *British Society of Scientific Glassblowers*, 24 St Michael's Avenue, Houghton Regis, Dunstable, Bedfordshire LU5 5DN; *Glass and Glazing Federation*, 44-48 Borough High Street, London SE1 1XB. Tel: 020-7403 7177. Fax: 020-7357 7458.

See also: Locksmith, blacksmith.
Find out about: Glazier.

Graphologist

We all have our own unique style of handwriting. In fact it is so distinctive that an expert can tell a lot about you from the way you write. The study of a person's character or personality from handwriting is called graphology. This is possible even though many of us are taught a similar style of handwriting as children. As we grow older our natural instincts change the way we write. Far from being a hobby graphology is an important tool in many big businesses who use graphologists to help them choose the right people to employ. Graphology is also used in child and family guidance and to help people decide what job they are best suited to. There is also a branch of graphology concerned with therapy through handwriting called *graphotherapy*.

You need to have a good understanding of psychology as well as expert knowledge of handwriting styles and what they mean. However, anyone prepared to apply themselves can learn and you can study and work at graphology from home.

74

● **How many graphologists are there?** There are about 200 graphologists in the UK, but probably only six who are top class. However, there are hundreds of students and hobby graphologists.

● **Job prospects and pay** Your prospects as a graphologist are not great and the handful of professionals are usually supported full-time by their partners. There is no career structure - you will have to find your own clients and charge what you think you are worth. One leading graphologist with corporate and celebrity clients charges £300 per hour.

● **Start-up costs** Your major costs will be training which is very expensive. You will also need to buy books and pay for travel to conferences and lectures.

● **How old must you be?** There are no official age limits. However, a teacher of graphology of many years standing considers that maturity is needed because you need experience of life and knowledge of psychology.

● **Training** You need to devote a few hours each week to study. A minimum starter course at the *British Institute of Graphologists* takes about three years. Many important books on the subject are written in French or German although more are being written in English. The *London College of Graphology* runs a three-year course.

● **Qualifications** You do not need any qualifications to work in the UK, but the *British Institute* awards its own qualifications up to diploma level (MBIG). The Institute can also provide information about qualified members who offer other forms of tuition such as private lessons or correspondence courses.

Contacts: Secretary, *British Institute of Graphologists*, 134 Netley Lodge, 134 Old Woking Road, Woking, Surrey GU22 8NY. Tel: 01932-354129 (Information pack for 38p SAE). Website: **www.britishgraphology.org**; *London College of Graphology*, Tel: 020-8876 5338/020-8392 1900.

See also: Calligrapher, bookbinder.
Find out about: Counsellor, psychologist.

Greetings card writer   £ – £ £

The verses or sayings inside greetings cards either make you squirm or make you think 'I can do better'. Whether you like or loath them greetings cards are big business and the companies that produce them have a huge appetite for appropriate words to go in them. If you think that you have a winning way with words and the necessary wit and imagination to write greetings card words then have a go.

Humorous verse or punch lines are sought after, but these are very hard to write. You have to master the technique of making your point in very few words. If you can write humorously then your chances of success are much higher.

Many of the major card companies have their own staff writers, but there are always opportunities for freelance writers to make their mark. Look for the names of companies on cards of the kind you would like to write for or contact the *Greetings Card Association* with an A5 SAE and they can provide a list of members prepared to look at freelance work - that is 50-60 out of 90 companies.

Approach companies with suitable work in batches of about 20. Give each separate price a reference number so you can track its progress. Put your copyright notice on each piece of paper. Include your contact details and a SAE for return of work. Send your work to a particular individual in the company with a covering letter. Remember that most companies receive about 30 requests a week from budding writers so you need to be good!

● **How many greetings card writers are there?** There are very few freelance card writers because of the prevalence of staff writers. To become a staff writer you need to apply to companies directly and are more likely to have had some other training, such as PR or journalism.

● **Job prospects and pay** If you can produce the work to the companies' satisfaction and get regular work you can earn a reasonable amount. The average payment is about £5 a line.

• **Start-up costs** There are no specific start-up costs, but you will look more professional if you use a PC. You will also need reference books such as the *Writers and Artists Yearbook* or *The Writer's Handbook*.

• **How old must you be?** You can be any age.

• **Training** There is no particular training as it depends on your talents.

• **Qualifications** No qualifications are necessary although you might want to take general writing classes at your local adult education centre.

Contact: *Greetings Card Association*, 41 Links Drive, Elstree WD6 3PP. Tel/Fax: 020-8236 0024.

See also: Calligrapher.
Find out about: Author, poet, journalist, copywriter.

Horologist (watchmaker)   £ – £ £

None of us can get by without some means of telling the time. But we tend to take clocks and watches for granted whether a basic wristwatch or the town hall clock. If you are fascinated by the mechanics of time and like making things work then consider horology as a career. For someone who likes taking things apart and mending them horology can be fascinating. However, you also need to be patient and have an eye for detail. Alternatively you might be excited by the idea of creating a watch or clock from start to finish including designing the casing. There is room in the profession for all types of practitioner.

You can work with a jeweller, with a Master, for a clock and watch company, for a retailer, or become self-employed. If you become self-employed you can choose the kind of work you do. It is a job full of variety; you might find yourself climbing a church tower to give the church clock its annual check, or on another occasion sitting at your bench repairing the inside of a tiny antique wristwatch.

The work can involve repairing or making watches and clocks. There is more demand for watch repairers than clock repairers and most work is in this field. Related skills might involve dating antique clocks and watches, designing new clocks, training others and writing on horological subjects.

● **How many horologists are there?** Nobody knows, because most professional technicians don't belong to a trade organisation.

● **Job prospects and pay** There is always a demand for watch repairers, especially people who can mend old watches and clocks. Jewellers from all over the country need people who can repair watches. You would normally work full-time for a jeweller. If you are prepared to travel to another part of the country your job prospects increase. The best prospects are as a self-employed horologist. But you would need to provide proof of your experience before retailers would trust customers with you. You can earn about £60 per week at 16 and £110 when qualified.

● **Start-up costs** If you want to start you own business you will need capital of about £10,000 for the necessary machinery and basic spares. You will get together the usual hand tools during training.

● **How old must you be?** In theory age doesn't matter, but employers prefer younger people because low wages are offered to inexperienced people. Different grades of watches need different levels of experience to repair them so the wages vary. But self-employment is an option with no age barriers.

● **Training** There are several colleges in the UK that offer full- and part-time courses in Technical Horology. These involve three years of study, the submission of a portfolio of work and exams.

The *British Horological Institute (BHI)* provides several other methods of gaining an internationally recognised qualification in horology. The BHI provides correspondence courses at three levels, Preliminary, Intermediate and Final. It also has an apprenticeship scheme for people under 21. This involves working full-time with a Master while undertaking formal qualifications to gain professional qualifications. If you don't have much money you can apply for grant assistance from the BHI.

• **Qualifications** You don't need any specific qualifications to become a watchmaker under the BHI training schemes. But for entry to colleges you will need to satisfy the usual college entrance requirements as set out in their prospectuses.

Contacts: *British Horological Institute* (BHI), Upton Hall, Upton, Newark, Nottinghamshire NG23 5TE. Tel: 01636-813795. Fax: 01636-812258. E-mail: clocks@bhi.co.uk. Website: **http://www.bhi.co.uk**; *School of Horology*, City College Manchester, Arden Centre, Sale Road, Northenden, Manchester M23 0DD. Tel: 0161-957 1500. Fax: 0161-945 3854; *School of Horology*, UCE, Perry Barr, Birmingham B42 2SU.

See also: Antiques restorer, locksmith.
Find out about: Bookbinder, engineer, model maker, technical illustrator.

Hot air balloon pilot   £ – £ £ £ £ £

In spite of the publicity given to ballooning, the round the world balloon winners and Richard Branson, ballooning is not a modern sport. It started in the eighteenth century when D'Ariandes and de Rozier piloted over Paris a hot air balloon built by the Montgolfier brothers. Shortly after that hydrogen was proved to be an effective lifting medium, but it was not until the 1950s that true hot air ballooning was revived. Today hot-air balloons rival hydrogen filled balloons by 500 to one. Modern hot air balloons, however, use bottled liquid petroleum gas to produce the heat.

Warm air rises and because warm air is lighter than the surrounding air it can lift a balloon if enough of it is trapped inside. When the air cools the balloon gently descends. You will not wear parachutes or seat belts, but the safety record for ballooning is equal to that of the major airline carriers. All safety features are duplicated and even a peck from a bird is not going to deflate the balloon - it already has a huge hole at the base for the air! There are no complicated electronics to go wrong. The fuel stands in containers in the corners of the basket and there are padded covers around them.

Balloons can carry any number of people from one to about 50, depending on their size. Large balloons are used by commercial operators to carry fare-paying passengers while an average balloon will carry the pilot and a couple of other people. It takes four people to launch a balloon. Women do just as well at ballooning as men.

As a pilot you can work for a commercial organisation or else buy and pilot your own balloon either as a commercial venture or to enter races for prize money.

● How many hot air balloon pilots are there? Surprisingly only 25% of the *British Balloon and Airship Club (BBAC)* members are pilots.

● Job prospects and pay Your best chance of earning a living from ballooning is by carrying paid passengers on trips and by attracting a sponsor.

● Start-up costs In order to pilot a balloon you need to pay for training. To buy your own balloon will cost you less than £8000. Running expenses will be £12-£15 per hour for fuel and maintenance plus a sum to cover annual maintenance. Don't despair if you haven't got that kind of money. Most balloons are owned by syndicates of between four to eight people. Sponsorship too can cover most of your expenses. Advertising on balloons is very popular with all kinds of companies because the public will go out of their way to look at balloons. 75% of all UK registered balloons carry advertising.

● How old must you be? The minimum age to qualify as a pilot is 17.

● Training It will take you from three to 12 months to train as a balloon pilot. You must complete a certain number of hours training in order to get your 'Private Pilot's Licence, Balloons and Airships'. You need a minimum of 16 hours flying instruction and then must take a check flight with a *Civil Aviation Authority (CAA)* appointed examiner. You also have to take four written exams. Further training is needed to gain a commercial licence if you want to make money from ballooning.

● Qualifications To pilot a balloon you need your 'Private Pilot's Licence, Balloons and Airships'. If you want to fly balloons for hire or reward you must obtain a Commercial Pilot's Licence.

Contacts: There is a great deal of information about ballooning on the Cameron Balloons website: **www.cameronballoons.co.uk/**; *British Balloon and Airship Club* (BBAC), Tel: 01604-870025. E-mail: info@bbac.org. Website: **www.bbac.org**; Civil Aviation Authority (CAA), CAA House, 45–59 Kingsway, London WC2B 6TE. Tel: 020-7379 7311. Fax: 020-7240 1153.

See also: Explorer
Find out about: RAF officer

Housekeeper   £ £ £ – £ £ £ £ £

Housekeeping is a worthwhile career. Looking after the needs of a house, whether large or small, needs good organisational skills, the ability to work well with other people and good communication skills. This has to be coupled with knowledge about how houses are run and how to do any of the jobs involved so that you can explain them to others. The job has advantages because you normally live-in and so board and lodging is provided.

Private households still employ housekeepers and typical employers that can afford to do so include the elderly or busy professionals such as doctors.

Most housekeepers live-in, but occasionally you can live-out. You can sometimes work as part of a couple if your husband is the gardener, chauffeur or handyman perhaps.

The other main employer of housekeepers are hotels. *The UK Housekeepers Association* regards professional housekeepers as those in hotels of over 30 bedrooms. The level of housekeeper you become depends on the size and quality of the hotel. If you become an executive housekeeper or housekeeping manager in a hotel in the four or five star range, with 50-1000 rooms, you would expect to manage a team of housekeeping staff.

● **How many housekeepers are there?** There are as many housekeepers as there are hotels with over 30 bedrooms, as well as those housekeepers working for private individuals. However, *The UK Housekeepers Association* has 600 members.

● **Job prospects and pay** After a solid foundation in housekeeping management at four or five star level you could move on to Front Office/front of House management positions. Your pay depends on the size, quality and location of the hotel and will be from £11,000 to £40,000. In three star hotels your job as a housekeeper would be very hands-on. When you move on to four or five start hotels you can be less hands-on because you will have more supervisory support. However, when there are staff shortages you will have to do your share of the work. Most housekeeping jobs are full-time especially when working for small private employers.

● **Start-up costs** None.

● **How old must you be?** Usually 18 or over.

● **Training** In hotels you need to get hands-on experience in various areas and then specialise as a floor housekeeper/deputy housekeeper.

When you reach deputy level it is vital to have specialist training in rostering/management, disciplinary and grievance handling, appraisal interviewing, interviewing skills, time management, budgeting, cost controls, team working and motivation.

● **Qualifications** It is possible to work your way up without any qualifications by learning on the job, but nowadays more and more employers prefer qualifications. You can get a degree in Hotel Management and later an NVQ level 4.

Contacts: Sheila Perera, Chairman, UKHA, The Gleneagles Hotel, Auchterarder, Perthshire PH3 1NF. Tel: 01764-694371.

See also: Butler, youth hostel warden.
Find out about: Bursar.

Indexer

£ £ – £ £ £

A good non-fiction book has a comprehensive and easy-to-use index. Finding the information you want without one can be time-consuming and frustrating. Often the index is the first part of the book that people turn to. Some writers produce their own indexes, but there is an art to creating a good index and this requires training. You need to be meticulous, methodical and capable of making informed judgements about the amount and type of information to include.

Once trained as an indexer you will usually be self-employed and hired by publishers. Although you will be able to index any books, most indexers specialise in a subject about which they have a good background knowledge. So, for example, you might do most of your work with theology, cookery or medieval history books. Indexers are rarely thanked by authors, but are a vital part of the team that produces a book. Most indexers are freelancers; others work for publishers in-house. You must be prepared to work at evenings and weekends to keep to tight deadlines. You must also be prepared to keep up with the times - web indexing and CD-ROM indexing are now part of an indexer's job.

You might love reading, but that alone is not enough to make you a good indexer. You need a good level of education and must be able to use language effectively. You must be very accurate and good at spelling, grammar and punctuation. It is not enough to rely on your word processor's spell checker.

● **How many indexers are there?** The *Society of Indexers* has 750 members, but not all indexers are members of the Society.

- **Job prospects and pay** Publishers always need good indexers, but it may take some time before you can get enough work to make indexing a career. You might want to combine it with other work until you are established. Trained and qualified indexers have a better chance of getting work. The pay is usually by the hour with the present (1999) recommended minimum rate being £14 per hour. More experienced indexers or those dealing with complicated text can charge more. Suitably qualified indexers are listed in the Society's *Indexers Available* which is distributed to publishers each year.

- **Start-up costs** If you train with the *Society of Indexers* you will pay £223 as a Society member and membership of the Society costs £40 a year. You will also need a good computer and word processing software, specialised indexing software costing about £400 and preferably e-mail, answer machine and fax facilities. So the total outlay will be about £2000.

- **How old must you be?** You can learn to index at any age and many indexers are late starters or turn to indexing as a second career.

- **Training** Ideally you should train with the *Society of Indexers*. The course consists of five training units (modules) and five corresponding tests. The exams can only be taken by Society members - so a first step to indexing is obviously to join the Society!

- **Qualifications** No specific qualifications are necessary, but completing the Society's course leads to their Accreditation status. You can later have your experience and competence assessed by the Society's assessment procedure and achieve Registered status.

Contact: *Society of Indexers*, Globe Centre, Penistone Road, Sheffield S6 3AE. Tel: 0114-281 3060. Fax: 0114-281 3061. E-mail: admin@socind.demon.co.uk. Website: www.socind.demon.co.uk.

See also: Writers' agent, bookbinder.
Find out about: Copywriter, sub-editor.

Industrial photographer £ – £ £ £ £ £

Not all photographers are interested in portraits, landscape or news photography. Some prefer the challenging and rewarding career of industrial photography. If you are patient and can find beauty and interest in everything from machinery to factories then you might enjoy being an industrial photographer.

Industrial photography ranges from the boring to the exciting and can occasionally be dangerous. Your job will be to turn uninspiring objects or scenes into something exciting. A lot of the work involves providing photographs for annual reports, catalogues, brochures or other company literature as well as helping companies present their products in the best light.

You might be an all-rounder or choose to specialise in one aspect such as cars or heavy machinery. You will be expected to travel a lot in order to photograph products on location.

You can start a career in photography by being passionate about taking photographs, reading about and looking at the work of other photographers and gradually building up a portfolio of work. Once you have a good portfolio the first step is usually to apply to become a photographer's assistant. This requires patience and tenacity as you contact photographers whose work you like. You need to be reliable and willing to muck in with the day to day running of a studio. You will not be involved so much with taking photographs yourself, but helping the photographer to take his or her photos. Assisting in a studio will give you an insight into a photographer's life and you will possibly learn more here than a college can teach you. As you progress you can start taking your folio around to potential clients. Your first break will probably not pay much but will improve your portfolio. Always do your best work and gradually you will get more work as your name becomes known.

- **How many industrial photographers are there?** There are probably about 4000 photographers who are employed in commercial photography, which includes industrial photography.

- **Job prospects and pay** Many companies no longer have in-plant photography units so most industrial photographers are self-employed. Getting your first job is most difficult; after that the more your name gets known the more work you will be offered. Pay depends on the job and how much you can get.

- **Start-up costs** As industrial photography involves plant and processes photography and takes place on location you will need cameras, lighting, and transport. The cost will depend on how much you can afford and the system you are using. Always buy the best you can afford. Eventually you might want your own studio.

- **How old must you be?** There is no age limit. If you want to learn photography at college then the college age restrictions apply.

- **Training** You do not need any formal training and many photographers consider the best training they received was from assisting in a studio. There are courses at all levels from evening classes to degrees. Many colleges offer photography courses or photography as part of arts courses. A list of colleges affiliated to *The Association of Photographers* and information about becoming an assistant can be obtained by sending a SAE to the Association.

● **Qualifications** None are needed - you are judged solely by the standard of your work. However, the major photographic organisations including the *British Institute of Professional Photography* naturally encourage candidates to apply for their professional qualifications. Ideally you would not enter the industry until you had a formal period of training in photography. The institute considers the most effective course to be the Professional Qualifying examination which consists of an additional year following an HND or forms part of a degree programme.

Contacts: *The Association of Photographers*, 81 Leonard Street, London EC2A 4QS. Tel: 020-7739 6669. Fax: 020-7739 8707; *British Institute of Professional Photography*, Fox Talbot House, Amwell End, Ware, Hertfordshire SG12 9HN. Tel: 01920-464011. Fax: 01920-487056. E-mail: bipp@compuserve.com. Website: **www.bipp.com**.

See also: Ship's photographer.
Find out about: Picture researcher.

Jockey

Jockeys train and race horses for horse owners. To be a jockey you need to be able to ride as well as being of slight build and weight. You also need to be physically fit because you have to look after the horses and racing is physically hard work.

Some jockeys are self-employed; others are employed by stables and might be employed for other work besides riding horses. You might be employed by trainers of flat racing or National Hunt racehorses to ride at race meetings. It is possible to ride for more than one trainer.

There are two kinds of jockey - Flat Racing jockeys and Jump jockeys. Jockeys working their way up through the ranks are graded as Apprentice and Conditional. Before you can become a jockey you must work in a stable as an apprentice jockey or a stable hand. Only one in ten trainees are chosen to ride in races. The rest remain stable hands, but can rise to become head lad (even girls are called that!).

Your weight is certainly limited; for Flat Racing apprentices aged 16 the limits are 7-8 stone (44-51kg) for boys and 8-9 stone (51-57kg) for girls. There are slightly heavier limits for National Hunt apprentices.

- **How many jockeys are there?** There are about 550 jockeys in the UK, including Apprentices and Conditionals.

- **Job prospects and pay** An apprentice jockey or stable hand aged 19 with one years experience will earn about £140 per week. Apprentices and Conditional jockeys get their normal wage and half the riding fee when racing. The Flat Race Riding Fee is £63.35 and the Jump Riding Fee is £87.35. Racing jockeys' salaries vary according to their success rate. As well as the rate per ride they also receive about 7% of all prize money. In spite of this only the top 15 jockeys of either code are able to earn a decent living.

- **Start-up costs** The only start-up costs are the cost of a licence, about £150, and your riding equipment such as saddles, etc. The total cost would be about £400.

- **How old must you be?** You cannot ride on a racecourse until you are 16. Flat racing apprentices are aged 16-24 and National Hunt apprentices are aged 17-25.

- **Training** You get trained by the stable and take NVQs levels 1-3 in racehorse care and management. Any jockey wishing to ride must attend a four-day training course at the *British Racing School* before they ride. A nine-week course at the School is open to school leavers.

- **Qualifications** You don't need any qualifications, but must attend the courses at the *British Racing School.*

Contacts: Director, *The British Racing School*, Snailwell Road, Newmarket, Suffolk CB8 7NU. Tel: 01638-665103; *National Trainers Federation*, Website: **www.martex.co.uk/racehorsetrainers/indexmain.htm**; *The Jockeys Association of Great Britain Limited*, 39B Kingfisher Court, Hambridge Road, Dewberry, Berkshire RG14 5SJ. Tel: 01635-44102 or 41166. Fax: 01635-37932. E-mail: jockeys@jagb.co.uk.

See also: Zoo worker.
Find out about: Farm worker.

Landscape gardener   £ – £ £ £ £ £

Those of you who are keen gardeners or who like the idea of a career out of doors making gardens look beautiful might consider a career in landscape gardening.

Gardeners often learn their love of gardening as children, but many older people turn to gardening with a passion as a change from other jobs. Landscape gardeners do not just grow plants they design gardens as a whole and have to consider everything from fences to bushes, patios to lawns, and sheds to vegetable patches.

As a landscape gardener you discover your client's needs and also find out what budget they have for the project. You then draw up a plan showing all the elements in the garden as well as giving details of plants. You need to take into account the soil, climate and prevailing sun and wind. When required, you oversee the transformation, although some of your clients will prefer to do the work themselves.

You need to love gardening and be prepared to work long hours. You do not need to be good at art although an instinct for colour and form would be of help.

It is unusual nowadays to be employed as a landscape gardener for a large house. Rather it is more likely to be self-employed and work on both large and small projects as the occasions arise. Your job might be as small as designing a planting scheme for a small city garden or as large as designing the park for a municipal corporation.

● **How many landscape gardeners are there?** Because anyone can call themselves a landscape gardener it is impossible to estimate their numbers.

● **Job prospects and pay** You will get most of your work by word of mouth. You can design gardens for yourself and your friends and advertise in the local papers. Obviously if you have a qualification this will improve your chances of work. You can earn about £120-160 per week after training.

● **Start-up costs** You will need paper and pens, a tape measure, a camera and basic gardening tools.

● **How old must you be?** You can be any age, but if you want a qualification you will normally be 18 or over.

● **Training** Some local parks and colleges offer classes in basic gardening or landscape gardening. There are also correspondence courses and the *Open College of the Arts* will give instruction in landscape design. The *Royal Horticultural Society* provides lectures, demonstrations and courses in horticulture at all levels. At university level you can find courses in landscape architecture. There are also City and Guilds courses.

● **Qualifications** Although you don't need qualifications to become a landscape designer, clearly your clients will be more impressed if you have one. A general horticultural qualification, a degree in a related subject such as landscape architecture, or a certificate from a recognised correspondence course all help.

Contacts: *Royal Horticultural Society* - The Head of Education, The RHS Garden, Wisley, Woking, Surrey GU23 6QB; *Open College of the Arts* (OCA), Houndhill, Houndhill Lane, Worsborough, Barnsley. Tel: 01226-730495.

See also: Forest worker, gamekeeper, ecologist.
Find out about: Architect, town planner, florist.

Locksmith   £ £ – £ £ £

Lock making has been practised since the sixteenth century in Britain, but it was not then a mass trade. Most people used latches and with few possessions had little need to lock things away. As people moved into towns and manufacturing industries increased so the need for locks became greater. More people had money and documents that needed safe keeping. The late nineteenth century saw a boom in the locksmith trade. Even then much locksmith work was done on a small scale by whole families. Nowadays locks and keys are factory made, but the need for locksmiths remains. Who else can help you when you get locked out of your house?

Keys, of course, go hand in hand with locks and a locksmith must have an understanding of the mechanical processes by which a lock works.

A skilled locksmith not only makes locks but understands their different uses and also how to operate them. You not only sell locks and keys, but cut keys, repair locks, match and rekey locks, unlock the seemingly unlockable, and provide a service that covers all aspects of keys and locks. You can also offer an emergency service so that people who have been burgled, for example, can get their locks changed quickly. Another job is providing new locks for insurance purposes. You can give advice about all aspects of locksmithing. Today there are fewer skilled locksmiths than there used to be, because most locks are now assembled by semi-skilled labour.

• **How many locksmiths are there?** There are about 200 skilled locksmiths within the industry.

• **Job prospects and pay** The pay is good, but job prospects with large companies are poor. You can earn about £150+ per week. All locksmiths work full-time.

• **Start-up costs** If you are an independent locksmith you will need tools, materials and premises.

• **How old must you be?** 16+

• **Training** Training is usually on the job.

• **Qualifications** You should become a member of the *Master Locksmiths Association* as soon as you are professionally competent.

Contacts: *Master Locksmiths Association*, Units 4 & 5, Woodford Halse Business Park, Great Central Way, Woodford Halse, Daventry, Northants NN11 6PZ. Tel: 01327-262255. Fax: 01327-262539.

See also: Blacksmith, bookbinder.
Find out about: Engineer.

Mobility instructor for guide dogs
£ £ £ – £ £ £ £

A Guide Dog Mobility Instructor plays an important role in preparing both the dog and new owner for living together. Owners and guide dogs are matched carefully, but still need a period of adjustment so the best is achieved from the arrangement.

Puppies destined to be Guide Dogs spend a year with families ('puppy walkers') until they are used to home life. The dogs then spend six months at a Guide Dogs for the Blind Association Regional centre for training by guide dog trainers. It is after that that Guide Dog Mobility Instructors take over to give the dogs advanced training for four weeks. Trainers ensure that the dogs obey basic commands and receive more specialist training in such things as obstacle avoidance. Your job as mobility instructor is then to take over in the last few months before the dogs meet their owners and to teach the dogs more advanced guiding skills such as helping their handlers get through crowds safely. But your job does not finish once the dogs are given to their owners. Visually impaired owners and their dogs complete a month of extra training at a centre so that they get to know how to work with their animals. You teach the new owners to have confidence in their dogs and how to handle them correctly.

When the dogs are finally established in their homes you make periodic visits to provide support and resolve any problems.

● **How many mobility instructors are there?** 16-70 guide dog mobility instructors are taken on each year.

● **Job prospects and pay** An apprentice starts at about £13,576 rising to £19,540 on qualifying after a minimum of 37 months. There is a six months compulsory 'living in' period for new instructors with accommodation and food free. Employment is at Association Regional or smaller support centres. You can aim for promotion to supervisory or management posts.

● **Start-up costs** None.

● **How old must you be?** The minimum age is 18 and older entrants are encouraged.

● **Training** Training is a three year modular apprenticeship with the *Guide Dogs for the Blind Association*. On completion you get the Association's Guide Dog Mobility qualification.

● **Qualifications** You need 5 GCSEs/S Grades A-C(1-3) including English, Maths and a science subject. A GCSE social science subject is preferable. You must have a full driving licence and be experienced in handling dogs or other animals as well as experience of working with adults from various backgrounds.

Contact: *Guide Dogs for the Blind Association*, Hillfields, Burghfield Common, Reading, Berkshire RG7 3YG. Tel: 0118-983 5555. Website: **www.gdba.org.uk**.

See also: Zoo worker.
Find out about: Police dog handler.

Mountain guide   £ £ £ £ – £ £ £ £ £

Have you got a head for heights, nerves of steel and the ability to get on with people? If your idea of fun is clinging to a rock face by your fingers or trekking across difficult terrain, then a career as a mountain guide might be just the thing for you.

As a Mountain Guide you would lead groups to the highest and most remote mountains on earth. Or you might specialise in Alpine mountaineering or work with young people, women or senior climbers.

But you won't simply show people the way up mountains. Your work could involve a wide range of other activities. You might become one of the many Guides who instruct climbers either in groups or individually. Guides also teach and guide in snow and ice climbing, ski mountaineering and off-piste skiing. Or you might prefer to offer Sport climbing throughout Europe or in Britain instruct and guide on rock and indoor walls. You need to get on with people and ensure that whether you are leading walkers or climbers, everyone receives the same care and attention.

You might be asked to become a member of a mountain rescue team. It sounds glamorous and exciting, but it is tough and dangerous. People's lives will depend not only on how well you climb but also on how well you work in a team.

But a career as a mountain guide does not necessarily mean that you will spend all year in the mountains. You might become involved in equipment design, development and testing or act as a consultant or assist in filming. Perhaps you would lecture or write on mountaineering themes.

● How many mountain guides are there?
In 1997 there were over 3000 registrations for the Mountain Leader course, although not all of those qualifying will go on to qualify and work full-time as Mountain Guides.

● **Job prospects and pay** Prospects are good for qualified Guides. Most are self-employed and can expect to earn between £75-£200 a day. There is as much work as you can generate.

● **Start-up costs** You will need to buy and maintain basic mountaineering equipment.

● **How old must you be?** Before you can be considered for membership of the *British Association of Mountain Guides* you must be 22 or older and have fulfilled the Associations stringent mountaineering experience qualifications. You can register for training at 18, but usually have to be 20 to be assessed.

• **Training** You will face very strict training requirements because the people you lead will depend on you for their safety. Before you can become a British Mountain Guide you will be given rigorous training and assessment in all aspects of mountaineering and guiding. The qualification you achieve is the International Union of Associations of Mountain Guides (UIAGM) guide's license. This is the highest professional qualification recognised internationally for mountain and ski guiding. But expect training and assessment to take several years.

It is possible to start from scratch in mountaineering! Go out and climb with more experienced people. If you have friends who climb you could ask if they are willing to take you. Or look for courses to give you the skills you need. One place that offers a wide range of Mountaineering courses in general mountaineering and rock-climbing is Plas Y Brenin. Try to join a mountaineering club too. You can get experience in mountaineering while you are studying or working.

• **Qualifications** You don't need specific academic qualifications. But to apply for training as a British Mountain Guide must have extensive experience in summer rock-climbing, winter ice-climbing, summer and winter mountaineering, alpine climbing and ski-mountaineering. If you want to augment your guiding with work in outdoor centres, youth groups, schools, etc, consider adding some academic qualifications in related subjects such as geography, biology, geology or a teaching qualification.

Contacts: *British Association of Mountain Guides* (BMG), Capel Curig, Gwynedd LL24 0ET; *British Mountaineering Council*, 177-179 Burton Road, West Didsbury, Manchester M20 2BB. Tel: 0161-445 4747; Plas Y Brenin, Capel Curig, Gwynedd LL24 0ET. Tel: 01690-720214.

See also: Deep sea diver, explorer, hot air balloonist.
Find out about: Outdoor centre instructor, sports teacher.

Musical instrument maker

If you are skilled in woodwork, electronics or metalwork and love music you might enjoy becoming an instrument maker. There is a high demand for instruments and you might specialise in reproducing period instruments, organs or high quality orchestral instruments. (Digital equipment, pianos, guitars and many wind and string instruments are mass produced nowadays). You need some musical ability, at the least some ear for tuning. It is not necessary to be able to play an instrument in order to make one, but it obviously helps if you can.

If you are going to set up in business on your own, like all small business people you will need basic business and selling skills. You can get advice about this from the Crafts Council. You might prefer to work for a firm specialising in hand-crafted musical instruments such as De Beers.

● **Job prospects and pay** There is enough demand for hand made instruments of high quality to support a large number of people. Getting a job with a firm might be hard, but setting up on your own is always possible and the amount of work you get will depend on your skills and reputation. Your pay with a firm will be low until you are trained. After training you can earn about £170 per week.

● **Start-up costs** If you decide to become self-employed you will need the cost of your tools, materials and workplace.

● **How old must you be?** 16+

● **Training** Training is provided on the job through apprenticeship schemes. For older applicants training in related trades can be a good background. If you are interested in repairing modern electronic keyboard instruments then you need technical, engineering, design or programming level computer skills. A qualification in music technology is a good start. The Department of Communications and Music Technology at *London Guildhall University* offers courses of almost every aspect of musical instrument technology for the BTEC National Diploma and Higher Diploma which both last two years full-time, the City and Guilds certificate which is two years full-time and a BSc which is three years full-time. Other colleges also have full- and part-time courses in music technology. The *Institute of Musical Instrument Technology* awards a diploma and can provide further information.

● **Qualifications** There are no formal entry requirements. Three GCSEs is the minimum requirement. You can attend evening classes or learn from books, but customers and employers will be more impressed by a music technology qualification. For a BSc you will need the usual higher education entrance requirements. BTEC and City and Guilds will have other requirements.

Contacts: *Institute of Musical Instrument Technology*, 134 Crouch Hill, London N8 9DX; Crafts Council, 44A Pentonville Road, London N1 9BY. Tel: 020-7925 5000. Fax: 020-7837 6891. Website: **www.craftscouncil.org.uk**.

See also: Blacksmith, piano tuner.
Find out about: Cabinet maker, musician.

Forget about building ships out of matchsticks or plastic kits. Why not help create the real thing? Naval architects are engineers who are responsible for the design, construction and repair of both merchant and warships, and such things as drilling platforms, submarines, hover-craft, yachts, etc.

As a naval architect you work in a team. Your job is to co-ordinate the expertise of engineers in specialist disciplines and to take overall responsibility for the project. You need to have good managerial skills. At the same time you need to ensure that the final design is safe, eco-nomic and seaworthy. You also need to understand many different branches of engineering and be up-to-date with modern skills such as using computer aided design (CAD) and information technology (IT). You must to be able to co-ordinate the services of scientists, lawyers, business people and sea-going people of many kinds. You should be creative, enquiring, and logical and have good communication and leadership skills.

You normally specialise in one field or have a broader understand-ing of several fields. These are design, construction and repair, market-ing and sales, operations, regulation and surveying and overseeing, research and development, or education and training.

● **How many naval architects are there?** The *Royal Institution of Naval Architects (RINA)* has about 3300 members in the UK. Many of these will be in full-time education. A further approximately 2000 members live and work overseas. However, anybody can call themselves a naval architect, but will not necessarily be admitted to the RINA.

● **Job prospects and pay** Your job prospects will be good. As a RINA member you can register as a Chartered Engineer with the *Engineering Council* and the pay is therefore equivalent to Council pay according to the relevant grade.

● **Start-up costs** None, unless you set up your own studio.

● **How old must you be?** As a naval architect requires higher education you will normally be in your twenties.

● **Training** At A level you will need three subjects (or five Scottish Highers) including maths and physics. You then take a first degree in Engineering. If you take BTEC/SCOTVEC certificates and diplomas these might also allow you entry to BEng courses. If you cannot attend a BEng course you can satisfy the RINA's requirements by passing the Engineering Council's exams parts 1 and 2 or an approved profile of an OU degree.

The RINA also recognises technicians and for this post you need two years training and two years relevant experience following an ordinary degree, diploma or certificate. You can then register with the EC as an Incorporated Engineer (IEng) or Engineering Technician (EngTech) respectively, and become an Associate-Member of RINA. If your degree is not from an institution recognised by RINA you might be asked to gain additional training or experience.

You should join the RINA as soon as you are a student to register for training. This takes place after your degree and involves a minimum of two years with an accredited company scheme. This training will include design, engineering practice and management services. After training you will need to complete two years of responsible experience to become a full member.

● **Qualifications** You will need a BEng from an RINA approved institution.

Contacts: *Royal Institution of Naval Architects* (RINA), 10 Upper Belgrave Street, London SW1X 8BQ. Tel: 020-7235 4622. Fax: 020-7259 5912; *Engineering Council*, 10 Maltravers Street, London WC2R 3ER. You can get information about courses in naval architecture from the *Universities of Glasgow, College London, Newcastle upon Tyne, Southampton, Strathclyde* and *Plymouth Polytechnic, Southampton Institute of Higher Education* and the *City of Bath College of Further Education.* See any list of university addresses.

See also: Blacksmith.
Find out about: Engineer.

Out-of-print book finder

You can start a career as an out-of-print bookfinder from your home. All you need is a love of books, a readiness to travel and an eye for spotting what your customers need. The job has something of the thrill of a detective story as you follow clues and hunt out books that may not otherwise see the light of day. Your hunting grounds will be second hand book shops, companies dumping the last copies of out-of-print books, private individuals selling their collections and anywhere where books can be found.

When books go out of print, there are often people who need or want a copy and are willing to pay for you to find it. You hunt the book down and then offer it to your client at a profit on your purchase price and the cost of postage. Normally you do not insist that customers buy the book if they change their minds or consider the price too high. You would not buy the books until your client had confirmed they will buy. You reserve the book at the bookseller for a short period. As you get known to booksellers they will help you find books and point you towards other sources. You will need to arrange to get catalogues from any likely second-hand booksellers.

Nowadays many books are sold through the Internet or by e-mail so you need to have a good command of IT and consider producing your own web page to attract customers. Certainly your records must be up to date, so a computer is vital. It is a job that can be done full- or part-time and you would be self-employed.

You will do better if you specialise in one area of books, such as travel or history.

● **Job prospects and pay** It depends on how much time and effort you give to the job. For many people it is a part-time source of income; others, perhaps with a partner, operate full-time.

● **Start-up costs** You need a computer and modem and the usual office equipment.

● **How old must you be?** Any age you like.

● **Training** You don't need any training, but you must know about the history of books and publishers. You can teach yourself this.

● **Qualifications** None needed.

Contacts: Make your own contacts with booksellers and publishers.

See also: Bookbinder, private detective, genealogist.
Find out about: Author, editor, picture researcher.

Patent agent/patent attorney

A patent is a grant by the State that gives a person the sole right to an invention or device for a specific number of years. It cannot just be a new way of doing something; it must have a mechanical or practical basis. Once someone has a patent for the invention he or she can stop other people using the invention for up to 20 years.

Patent agents are specially trained to draft patents and have a detailed knowledge of intellectual property law. You help your employer or client to protect their innovations and developments and advise them about the property rights of others. You can also call yourself a patent attorney although sometimes solicitors can use the term even if they have not passed any exams relating to intellectual property. A job related to patent agent is that of trade mark agent. A trade mark agent deals with all aspects of trade mark law.

As a patent agent you are involved with drafting, presenting and obtaining patents. You need to be able to understand the technical side of inventions in order to explain them properly. But your job is not confined to this. You also deal with the wider aspect of intellectual property, trade marks, design, copyrights and so on. You could spend time informing your client or employer of major licensing or acquisitions, advising your clients on new products to develop, or helping them improve their market edge.

Most patent agents are employed in private practice often representing and advising UK industry or foreign countries. Less than half the patent agents in the UK are employed by the government or directly in industry.

Most patent agents or attorneys deal with scientific based intellectual rights, but you will need to know about literary or musical and other artistic copyright matters.

Because you are involved with law, commerce and technology you need an understanding of scientific principles, the ability to write well and be a good communicator in order to mediate between inventors, lawyers, bureaucrats and the Patent Office. The Patent Office is an executive agency of the Department of Trade and Industry.

● **How many patent agents are there?** There are 1350 qualified patent agents on the Register of Patent Agents.

● **Job prospects and pay** The salary during training is usually fair - about £13,000. Newly qualified you earn about £20,000 and patent examiners can earn much more.

- **Start-up costs** None.

- **How old must you be?** Most agents have a degree so you will be in your twenties.

- **Training** You do not need a degree to be a patent agent, but most new entrants have a degree or the equivalent. It is almost impossible to practise in the UK without being a European Patent Attorney and the European Patent Office stipulates a degree or equivalent in a technology-based subject. You need to train for several years either in private practice or within an industrial department to pass the professional examinations of the *Chartered Institute of Patent Agents (CIPA)*. You can get exemption from some foundation examinations by taking courses run by Queen Mary and Westfield College.

- **Qualifications** It takes between four and six years to qualify as a Chartered Patent Agent. To qualify as a European Patent Attorney you need to have trained for at least three years under the supervision of a European Patent Attorney and pass the European Qualifying Examination. It is illegal to practice as a patent agent unless you are on the official list of qualified practitioners, that is the Register of Patent Agents.

Contacts: Chartered Institute of Patent Agents (CIPA), Staple Inn Buildings, High Holborn, London WC1V 7PZ. Tel: 020-7405 9450. Fax: 020-7430 0471. E-mail: mail@cipa.org.uk. Website: **www.cipa.org.uk**.

See also: Private detective.
Find out about: Inventor, lawyer.

Personal shopper   £ – £ £ £

You know the feeling - you have a wardrobe full of clothes and not a thing to wear. Or you're going to that important party or conference and need to look the part. Or maybe you just need a change of look but are unsure of what clothes suit you.

Men and women often need a helping hand to choose clothes that suit them. Or they know the kind of thing they want but haven't got the time to choose it themselves. This is where personal shoppers come in.

You either work for yourself or a big store. Those who work for stores are often recruited from existing employees. If you are self employed you visit your client and discuss their clothing needs and arrange a time to go with them around the shops and help them choose their clothes. In a big store you accompany and advise shoppers or choose items for them and have them ready to choose from at a set time. In both cases you would keep details of clients' measurements, tastes, etc, so that you can help them again in the future.

● **How many personal shoppers are there?** Major stores in large cities might employ several personal shoppers each. It is impossible to calculate self-employed numbers because many combine their work with other jobs such as colour analysis.

● **Job prospects and pay** As a self-employed personal shopper you can charge what you think your clients can afford. If you are employed in a store your pay will be calculated according to company pay scales.

● **Start-up costs** None.

● **How old must you be?** 18+

● **Training** If you have an innate sense of style, colour and fashion you can go ahead without training. However, many personal shoppers have had training in related spheres such as colour analysis or art. If you work in a store you will be trained on the job.

● **Qualifications** None.

Contact: *Colour Me Beautiful*, FREEPOST, London SW8 3NS. Tel: 0845-603 3408. Fax: 020-7627 5680.

Pest control operator   £ £ – £ £ £

Most people dislike creepy crawlies and rodents, but some of these creatures are more than just unpleasant. They can spread disease or damage your home. If you are not afraid of them and want to do a job where you will be welcomed with open arms then become a pest control operator. By preventing and controlling pests such as rats, mice and cockroaches you are playing a vital role in maintaining public health.

Your main work might be stopping rats, mice, cockroaches and ants from damaging foodstuffs in hotels, factories, restaurants or private homes. But you might also be asked to deal with rabbits, moles, birds and foxes which attack farmers' crops. You could work for local authorities or private firms. You would be employed to set traps, lay poisons and so on. Graduate employees could work in research or management.

The work can be domestic, agricultural or commercial. Modern pest controllers are highly trained and need to be able to give advice as well as practical help. The law requires that everyone using pesticides is adequately trained and competent, but you do not have to be certified unless you are using pesticides classified for agricultural use. Nevertheless correct training is very important.

You can get into pest control by replying to ads in the local press by private press control contractors. Local authorities also have pest control activities so try applying to the Environmental Services Department. Once you have had some experience of pest control and its potential market you could become self-employed and run a pest control business from home.

This is not a job for you if you are squeamish. You need to take a mature attitude to humanely disposing of pests.

● **Job prospects and pay** School leavers start at about £8000. Graduates start at about £13,000.

● **Start-up costs** These only apply if you intend to set up as a private operator.

● **How old must you be?** 16+

● **Training** Training is on the job, but if you work for local government there are courses available. The *British Pest Control Association* provides training courses which are open to members and non-members alike. The courses include general pest control, fumigation, pricing for profit, controlling moles, rabbits and grey squirrels and working in confined spaces. You can also take exams for the BPC Diploma. There is now a level 2 Scottish National Higher qualification based on assessment and practical competence. The BCPA is accredited by City & Guilds and Scotvec.

● **Qualifications** Although you do not need qualifications it is clearly sensible to get them and you need them to work for a local authority. You can get a BPC diploma or the level 2 SNH qualification. You need a good general education with GCSEs including English and science subjects. If you want to progress to research or management you will need a biology or other relevant degree.

Contacts: *British Pest Control Association* (BPCA), 3 St James' Court, Friar Gate, Derby DE1 1BT. Tel: 01332-294288. Fax: 01332-295904. E-mail: enquiry@BCPA.org.uk. Website: **www. BCPA.org.uk**. Also ask local authorities whether they have any available jobs in pest control.

See also: Gamekeeper.
Find out about: Damp course installer, gas fitter, electrician.

Piano tuner   £ £ – £ £ £

You don't have to be blind to be a piano tuner, but it can help. The job is so reliant on the sensitivity of the ears that blind people with their heightened sense of hearing make good piano tuners.

But anyone with a good musical ear and patience can learn to be a piano tuner. You don't have to be able to play the piano although obviously you need a knowledge of the way a piano works and the range of notes.

Pianos are affected by temperature - they do not like to be too hot or cold. So central heating plays havoc with a piano's tuning. The action and keys are the playing mechanism of the piano and if these wear out or are not properly regulated then the performance of the piano is diminished.

You could find yourself tuning a old upright piano in a pub, a small modern piano in a private home or a grand piano in a concert hall. All kinds of places have pianos that need regular tuning - schools, pubs, halls, etc. How often you regulate or tune a piano depends on its quality and the environment it is kept in. So you might tune individual pianos on anything from a monthly to a five yearly basis. Home-based pianos are usually tuned once or twice a year. Concert and musicians' pianos are dealt with more frequently.

You will need to be able to dismantle a piano and tune it and also diagnose other faults even if you do not fix them yourself. Sometimes all that is needed is a good clean - my piano tuner swears by WD40!

• **How many piano tuners are there?** Many piano tuners are self employed so numbers are hard to estimate.

• **Job prospects and pay** A good piano tuner will be in demand and you will make more money as your client list grows. A starting salary might be £150-£170 per week. If you are self-employed you can earn up to £400 per week when you become well-established.

• **Start-up costs** You will need your tuning tools and, if you do not have perfect pitch, a tuning fork or electronic tuner.

• **How old must you be?** The minimum age for training is 16.

• **Training** You can teach yourself especially if you have perfect pitch and a good knowledge of pianos. But a better way is to train in a reputable factory or workshop for at least three years or gain a recognised qualification. You are advised to obtain a National Diploma in Musical Technology which gives a basic two-year training in tuning and repairing upright pianos. You can then go on to a HND in Musical Technology or a BSc(Hons) Music Technology. For these latter courses you must be 18 and suitably qualified. The HND is particularly suitable as it focuses on repairs, tuning and restoration, moving from uprights to grands. Various colleges run training courses in piano tuning and repair and they are listed below.

• **Qualifications** You do not need any qualifications, but you would be unlikely to be able to work effectively as a piano tuner unless you have had some basic training. A ND in Music Technology is therefore the basic qualification you need. Once you have completed either three years recognised training in a factory or workshop or gained a recognised qualification as a piano tuner or technician and done practical training you can join the *Pianoforte Tuners' Association*. Or if you have earned your living as a piano tuner for seven years you can join.

Contacts: *The Pianoforte Tuners' Association*, E-mail: members@pianotuner.org.uk. Website: **www.pianotuner.org.uk/**; Faculty Registry, *Sir John Cass Faculty of Arts, Design and Manufacture*, London Guildhall University, 41 Commercial Road, London E1 1:A. Tel: 020-7320 1827. Fax: 020-7320 1830 (ND, HND, BSc Hons);Customer Services, *Newark & Sherwood College*, FREEPOST (NG61636), Newark, Notts NG24 4BR. Tel: 01636-705921. Fax: 01636-701990 (City & Guilds); Deputy Head of Creative Arts, *The Royal National College for the Blind*, College Road, Hereford HR1 1EB. Tel: 01432-265725. Fax: 01432-353478 (ND for Piano Tuners); Head of MIT Section, *Stevenson College*, Carrickvale Annexe, Stenhouse Street West, Edinburgh E11. Tel: 0131-443 8888 X29.

See also: Musical instrument maker, locksmith, blacksmith, horologist.
Find out about: Musician.

Political party agent (constituency agent) £ £

A political party constituency is an area served by an MP. The person who is responsible for running the constituency efficiently is the constituency agent. He or she checks the electoral registers, arranges membership and fund-raising drives, organises meetings and MPs' visits and generally deals with local party matters.

Not all constituencies have agents and the position can be paid or unpaid. However, your helpers are normally voluntary. You can work as an agent at local, regional or national party level. The job is hard work but is regarded as good training should you eventually want to become an MP.

● **How many political party agents are there?** There is usually at least one for each political party for each constituency.

● **Job prospects and pay** You can start at local level and end up working for a political party as an agent at national level in the party headquarters.

● **Start-up costs** None.

● **How old must you be?** Normally 18.

● **Training** Each political party has different training requirements, but all parties have specific training for agents that must be undertaken before you are eligible to act as an agent. The best way to start is to volunteer.

● **Qualifications** You need to be a member of the political party and to have been a member for a specific amount of time. You need to have good organisational skills and the ability to organise volunteers. Your party might require you to sit exams related to agency work.

Contacts: Contact the local political party of your choice (the address will be at your local library).

See also: Tour guide.
Find out about: MP.

Potter   £ – £ £

Remember those coil pots you made in school? If you liked making them and feel you want to progress to thrown pots then you could become a potter.

Although you can sell coil pots, thrown pots are more usual. A lump of wet clay is thrown onto the centre of a moving horizontal solid wheel and you pull the clay towards you with both hands shaping the pot between your hands. You turn the wheel using a foot lever or electrically. Pots, of course, can be any shape or size, from a small cup to a gigantic garden urn.

You can then decorate the pot using slip, a creamy layer of wet clay used for coating, decorating and casting pottery. Pots are fired in kilns and then decorated or can be decorated and then fired.

Many potters are self-employed and work from their homes. Others work in potteries designing and making pots on a commercial scale.

You need to love using your hands and have a natural feel for using clay. An artistic flair helps, of course, and you need to be a salesperson to sell your work.

● **Job prospects and pay?** The job prospects are what you make of them. A lot will depend on where you have your studio if you are self-employed - if, for example, there are other potters you will be competing with. Your earnings will be what you can get clients to pay. If you are employed in a pottery you could earn about £80 a week at 16.

● **Start-up costs** Unless you are employed by a factory you will need to buy a wheel, a kiln, clay, tools and decorating mediums, as well as hire or convert a studio space.

● **How old must you be?** Any age.

• **Training** You can teach yourself or go to adult education classes. In theory it takes about three years to learn to throw a pot. In practice you can learn to throw some form of pot in a few weeks - the expertise comes in making pots that look and feel good and learning how to fire and decorate them. You also need to become so proficient that you can create several pots all virtually identical.

• **Qualifications** Although you do not need any qualifications many potters have practical or art school training and have a degree or diploma in Art.

Contacts: Your local adult education institute, local art colleges, local, further and higher education colleges. Amateur and professional potters can join the *Craft Potters Association* (CPA), 21 Carnaby Street, London W1V 1PH. Tel: 020-7437 6781. Fax: 020-72879954. Website: **www.ceramic-review.co.uk/cpa/cpa.htm**.

See also: Bookbinder, sculptor, glass blower, antiques dealer.
Find out about: Woodworker.

Private detective   £ £

The Dick Marlow image still lingers in the mind of the public. The upstairs room, the man in the raincoat and hat trailing a suspect. In fact, as many recent television series have realised, many private detectives are now women and much of the work involves the less glamorous side of the life. So you might spend hours in cars logging the movements of errant spouses for divorce cases, tracing missing persons or serving writs.

You can work for an agency or be self employed. The work is varied and much of it is routine. You could be chasing debtors, finding witnesses and taking statements, video and photographic surveillance, e.g. in insurance company fraud, dealing with pre sue and means enquiries, verifying credit worthiness, investigating road traffic and individual accidents including making sketch plans and taking photos, land and property repossession and making test purchases.

Some private detectives are full-time, others work part-time or are self-employed. Some are ex-police officers; many are not. But if you are prepared for the hours of boredom and mundane aspects of the job then you might enjoy being a private detective.

• **How many private detectives are there?** Nobody knows the answer to this one - and they wouldn't tell you anyway!

• **Job prospects and pay** You earn what people are prepared to pay. The job prospects are what you make of them. You can work for an agency and when you have learned the job you can set up on your own. Your pay will depend on your age and experience. Working self-employed you can earn £25-£30 per hour but might charge clients on a set fee basis. Remember, much of it will go towards basic expenses such as rent, phone bills, etc.

● **Start-up costs** These are the same as for any small business needing to rent office space and equipment. Obviously a phone, answer machine and mobile phone are vital. You need to pay for personal indemnity and public liability insurance and register with the Office of Fair Trading and the Data Protection Registrar.

● **How old must you be?** There are no age restrictions, but common sense should tell you that anyone under eighteen is unlikely to get work.

● **Training** You do need a lot of training for this kind of work. Without police training you will need to train on the job. Extra training in self defence and law will also be useful. However, you should be of good standing and have a sound knowledge of computers and experience in credit control or experience of working in a service industry meeting the public. You can attend training seminars run by the *Association of British Investigators*.

● **Qualifications** You don't need any qualifications for this job, but NVQs levels 3 and 4 are available in investigation techniques. You must also be honest and have integrity. You need to be discrete, patient, persevering, able to work alone, outgoing and adaptable.

Contacts: Association of British Investigators, ABI House, 10 Bonner Hill Road, Kingston-upon-Thames, Surrey KT1 3EP. E-mail: abi@globalnet.co.uk. Website: **www.assoc-britishinvestigators.org.uk**. Look for local agencies who might take you on as a trainee.

See also: Genealogist, researcher, bailiff.
Find out about: Security guard.

Puppeteer   £ – £ £ £ £ £

Is Punch and Judy your idea of a good afternoon's entertainment? Do you enjoy making models and acting? Then why not be a puppeteer? You could be involved in everything from making the puppet - hand, string, or rod puppets - making and designing the stage and sets, writing and performing. You would probably be self-employed and work part-time. Puppeteers range from amateurs, semi-professional to fully professional. There are some full-time professional puppetry companies, but job prospects with them are very limited.

Puppeteers entertain at private parties, in theatres, for schools and at seaside resorts - in fact anywhere where puppets are appreciated.

● **How many puppeteers are there?** Many puppeteers do not belong to any of the Puppetry Support Organisations (PSOs), puppetry organisations or Equity, so numbers are unknown.

● **Job prospects and pay** Talented full-time puppeteers living in an area where there is a demand for puppet shows obviously earn more than those who are semi-professional. Pay varies between places, companies, and people, but might be anything from £20 to £250 a day.

● **Start-up costs** These will depend on whether the company has more than one person, the size and complexity of your rig and how technical you are. The very least you need is a puppet!

● **How old must you be?** You can be a puppeteer at any age.

● **Training** You need to have skills such as manipulating, performance, physical theatre, mime, voice and singing depending on how you want to work. Many puppeteers also have practical craft skills such as carving or costume design and for these you would need training either in classes or from an expert. Joining a puppetry organisation such as BrUNIMA can advise you about further training. *The Puppet Centre* promotes national and international training opportunities.

● **Qualifications** The only qualifications you need are skills and experience so go for it!

Contacts: Membership Secretary, BrUNIMA, 10 Cullernie Gardens, Balloch, Inverness IV2 7JP; *British Puppet & Model Theatre Guild*, 65 Kingsley Avenue, West Ealing, London W13 OEH. Tel/Fax: 020-8997 8236; *The Puppet Centre*, BAC, Lavender Hill, London SW11 5TN. Tel: 020-7228 5335. Website: **www.toy.co.uk/associations/puppet-centre/index.htm**.

See also: Embroiderer, wardrobe master/mistress.
Find out about: Doll maker.

Racing driver   £ – £ £ £ £ £

You probably think of racing drivers as the drivers of Formula 1 cars racing around a racetrack. You may long for the exhilaration and the test of your skill and nerve. But remember that driving a racing car is not like driving an ordinary car.

There are other opportunities for racing and each year there are over 200 race meetings which will give you the opportunity to race a wide range of cars from ordinary saloons to single-seaters. There are two kinds of motor sport - those where cars compete against each other directly, as in circuit racing, and events where cars compete alone and where timing may or may not be important.

A good way to start in racing, for younger people, is by karting and many famous Formula 1 champions were successful kart racers.

The sport is still dominated by men, but it is open to women and many more women are participating. Women in racing are supported by the British Women Racing Driver's Club. Disabled drivers too are encouraged and each case is assessed individually. It is usually easier for a disabled person to get a licence for competing singly or at a lower speed.

If you want to be a racing driver your first step should be to join a motor club which is recognised by the British governing body for motor sport, the RAC Motor Sports Association (MSA). Contact the relevant regional organisation for details of your most suitable local club. Depending on your level of expertise you might want to start by accompanying other drivers in races that require a passenger to be present. You can then think about buying or building your first car. You will probably only need your club membership card for most races, but if you want to compete outside your club you must get a RACMSA licence. You can then compete in the races to gain experience. Only the lucky few ever get taken on by sponsors to race professionally.

● **How many racing drivers are there?** About 30,000 people hold RACMSA competition licences and there are about 100,000 competitors altogether, although few earn their living from the sport.

● **Job prospects and pay** You are more likely to get employment as a support worker such as a truck driver, mechanic, engineer, tyre fitter, electrician, salesperson, secretary or in the PR or administration side. You could start off in this way and race on the side. To earn money from racing driving you need to find a sponsor who is willing to take on most of the costs and pay you. As you can imagine job prospects for drivers are few.

● **Start-up costs** Start-up costs for a racing driver are considerable. Even if you decide to race your own car, you will need to buy an RACMSA competition licence starting with a novice licence and pack (£37) and half a day's training (£150). You then need your racing kit of gloves, helmet, overalls, etc (£200-£500). Club race fees could cost you about £1300 for 12 races and you will need about £2000 a year for running costs. If you want to buy a car it could cost you anything from £1500-£15,000. Cars usually come up for sale at the end of the season. Or you could save some money and build a car yourself. Once you have bought a car you will also need safety equipment such as fire extinguishers, fire-proofing, etc.

● **How old must you be?** Anyone over the age of eight can drive competitively, starting with karting, but to be a racing driver you must be at least 17 and hold a valid RTA Driving Licence or 16 with at least one year's experience in karting. If you are over 18 you need a medical certificate too. All the information is in the RACMSA 'Go racing' starter pack.

● **Training** Start by karting and then move onto competition car racing at your local club. To get your novice licence you must undertake a compulsory half day's training at one of the *Association of Racing Drivers' Schools (ARDS)*.

● **Qualifications** If you have not already got a Race Licence you must first apply to the RACMSA for a 'Go racing' Pack which contains among other things information about how to obtain a Race National B licence which allows you to race in the UK. Other licences allow you to race throughout the EU or internationally.

Contacts: *RAC Motor Sports Association* (MSA), Motor Sports House, Riverside Park, Coinbrook, Berkshire SL3 0HG. Tel: 01753 681736. Fax: 01753-682938. E-mail: racmsa@compuserve.com. *Website:* www.ukmotorsport.com/; *British Motor Sports Association for the Disabled* (BMSAD), PO Box 120, Aldershot, Hampshire GU11 3TF. Tel: 01252-319070; *Motor Sports Association* (MSA), 78 Ashleigh Gardens, Wymondham, Norfolk NR18 0EY. Tel: 01953-602916. Website: **www.autolinkuk.co.uk/bwrdc.**

See also: Courier, hot air balloonist.
Find out about: Train driver.

Radio DJ (disc jockey)   £ – £ £ £

The traditional way of becoming a DJ is to practise at home or by DJ-ing in your local discos, pubs or hospital. Then send a tape of your technique to local radio stations and hope for the best.

What do DJ's do? They choose and play the music, ensure that breaks are taken for any ads or news and chat to the listeners. Nowadays they might also interview people or take phone-in comments. They are the key to a successful and smooth running music programme. You need to be able to talk to the audience and hold their attention by thinking of new things to say. You also have to keep a sensible balance between music and chat.

You may be lucky in trying to enter the job in this way, but most DJs on radio have had some experience either on a media studies course or through working elsewhere on radio programmes while waiting for a break. There is a lot of luck in this job.

A good way to start is to offer your services free to a community radio such as your local hospital radio. You will not only be gaining valuable experience, but will be doing something worthwhile.

● **Job prospects and pay** Your pay will depend on your work and hours. Famous DJs get paid a great deal. Your job prospects will depend on your persistence and experience.

● **Start-up costs** If you are DJ-ing locally to get experience you might need turntables, CDs, tapes and recording equipment.

● **How old must you be?** There is no age limit.

● **Training** A media studies course with a practical radio element might be helpful, but the best way to train is to get experience. You can start by helping an established local DJ and then branch out on your own before applying to radio stations. Any radio experience you can get will be useful, from school radio upwards. Then make a tape to show what you can do and send copies to local radio stations.

● **Qualifications** There are no actual qualifications, but a pleasant speaking voice, a quick wit, confidence and loads of ideas are essential. You need to have a broad knowledge and interest in individual bands and the music scene as a whole. You should naturally be a good communicator and have a lively enquiring mind.

Contacts: Details of local and national radio stations can be found in *The Writer's Handbook* (Macmillan, annually) and *Writers' and Artists' Yearbook* (Black, annually).

See also: Comedian.
Find out about: Radio journalist, holiday camp compere.

Reflexologist ···£ £

Every part of your body is connected by energy pathways which end in specific areas on the feet, hands and head. Reflexologists believe that by stimulating specific points they can help a patient relax, improve balance and heal themselves. So, for example, treating the big toe has a related effect in the head. The pressure on reflexology points stimulates the body to achieve its own natural state of wholeness and good health.

If this sounds like the kind of medicine that you think is effective then you might think about a career in reflexology.

You need to be a good communicator because treatment involves preliminary talk with the patient. Then the patient removes shoes and socks and you apply gentle pressure with your thumbs and fingers. The treatment lasts about an hour. Reflexology is becoming more popular as people try to eliminate the increased stress in their lives. You also need to be sensitive to people's feelings and a good listener.

• **How many reflexologists are there?** There are about 4500 members of the *Association of Reflexologists*. There are about 8000-10,000 reflexologists working in the UK.

• **Job prospects and pay** The job prospects are good as more people turn to complementary medicines. Most reflexologists in Britain work privately and you could charge between £15 and £20 an hour for treatment. Most reflexologists work part-time until they have built up their client base enough to support full-time working. More reflexologists are now being employed by the NHS, public companies, small businesses, hospices, care homes and clinics. Referrals might also come from private medical insurance companies or doctors.

• **How old must you be?** There are no maximum age limits, but some schools have a minimum age limit of 18.

• **Training** You should choose a course that has been accredited by the *Association of Reflexologists (AoR)*. Compare courses to find one whose approach suits you best. Although the courses are essentially practical they do include anatomy, physiology, biology, basic pathology and other areas such as first aid and management. You will also have to complete a number of case studies as well as written assignments, written examinations and practical assessments. Most accredited courses are part-time and last about 9 months. You can get a list of accredited schools from the AoR. Other courses are available but are not accredited by the AoR.

• **Qualifications** After successfully completing a course you will be awarded a practitioner's certificate.

Contacts: *Association of Reflexologists* (AoR), 27 Old Gloucester Street, London WC1N 3XX. Tel: 0870-5673320. E-mail: aor@reflexology.org. Website: **www.reflexology.org/aor**.

See also: Alternative medicine practitioner, chiropractor.
Find out about: Osteopath, physiotherapist, aromatherapist.

Researcher

When radio, TV or film producers, theatre directors, consumer magazines or writers want something investigated and the facts presented to them succinctly, they don't waste time themselves. They employ a researcher. This is the job for you if you enjoy investigating, researching in archives, interviewing people, searching on the Internet and generally finding facts by whatever means are necessary.

The work you do will depend on the kind of programme or play being produced or the book being written. Much of your work will be office-based, but you might also be asked to find the background on guests or interviewees, track down illustrations or film clips, research suitable topics, or interview prospective programme participants. The research might involve searching historical facts, tracking down a quotation, compiling a report on a particular subject - in fact finding out anything someone needs to know. This might be scientific or technical as well as literary or general knowledge so you need to have a broad understanding of many subjects even if you only specialise in one or two.

Once you have researched the facts or people as requested you then need to type up a report for your employer. For serious news programmes or factual books your job resembles investigative journalism.

The skills you need are persistence and patience and good writing and presenting skills as well as an inquiring mind. Nowadays you also need to have a good understanding of using computers as research tools. You must understand how libraries and archives work so that you make the best and most time-effective use of them. You need to be widely read so that you understand where a fact might be found.

Many researchers are freelance, but some are employed full- or part-time.

- **How many researchers are there?** This is difficult to answer because many researchers do other work too.

- **Job prospects and pay** There are not a great many full-time research jobs. Most work is on a contract basis per job. However, once you have established your reputation you can go freelance. Pay for full-time radio or TV researchers can be from £13-20,000, Freelance daily rates vary from £100-400.
- **Start-up costs** If you decide to be a freelance researcher you must have a computer and e-mail/fax facilities. Your main costs will be travel and the cost of specialist library tickets, photocopying or pictures.

- **How old must you be** Many researchers have had precious jobs, often in journalism or as editorial assistants.

- **Training** There is no specific training, but many researchers have trained in journalism, archive management or librarianship. There is an NVQ level 3 in Production Research available.

- **Qualifications** No specific qualifications are needed. A degree in any subject can be useful. To become a researcher you need to have a good knowledge of English and know where to look for things.

Contacts: The best indication of what a researcher does is to read the latest edition of *Research for Writers* by Ann Hoffman (A&C Black). Although written for writers it is written by an expert researcher and will give you an insight into what a researcher is required to do.

See also: Genealogist, private detective.
Find out about: Librarian, archivist.

Road rescue officer (patrol)　　£ £ – £ £ £

As a road rescue officer or patrol for the AA and the RAC you are the drivers' lifeline if their car or lorry breaks down. Your job is to respond to emergency calls day or night and to either fix the vehicle concerned or arrange for it to be taken to a garage for further work. Driver and passengers may also have to be provided with transport.

You will wear a uniform and drive either a van or motorbike in order to reach stranded vehicles quickly. Naturally you have to have a clean driving licence and be a very good motor mechanic. You also need to be a good communicator because you will be dealing with people who are stressed. You need to be able to follow directions and be good at map reading.

- **Job prospects and pay** Your pay is determined by whichever road rescue organisation you work for.

- **Start-up costs** Your uniform and emergency rescue vehicle are provided by the organisation.

- **How old must you be?** Normally 18+.

- **Training** Both the *AA* and *RAC* provide induction and ongoing training, but you need to have a proven background in the motor industry. There are full- and part-time courses and modern apprenticeships available for mechanics. ReMIT the training arm of the *Retail Motor Industry Federation* (RMIF) runs programmes of training courses at all levels. Older people can also train. NVQ levels 2 and 3 in Roadside Assistance and Recovery are currently being submitted for accreditation.

- **Qualifications** Preferably NVQs or City and Guilds qualifications in motor vehicle maintenance, mechanics or engineering.

Contacts: AA (Automobile Association), Norfolk House, Priestley Road, Basingstoke, Hants RG24 9NY; Website: **www.theaa.co.uk/**; RAC, Website: **http://www.rac.co.uk/**; Retail Motor Industry Federation (RMIF), 201 Great Portland Street, London WIN 6AB. Tel: 020-7307 3424. Fax: 020-7580 6376. Website: **www.rmif.co.uk/**.

See also: Courier, racing driver, classic car restorer.
Find out about: Taxi driver.

Saddler   £ – £ £

Making saddles, bridles and other leather gear for horse riders is a skilled traditional rural craft. You make all the kit needed to saddle a horse. This includes not only the saddle itself but the harness and bridle. The job mainly involves working with leather. You need to take into account not only the creation of the equipment, but the safety and comfort of both rider and horse.

But making bespoke saddles is only one opportunity open to you. You can become involved in retail or large scale trade manufacturing of saddles, predominantly based in Walsall. Only a minority of craft saddlers run workshops where they make their own saddles. A successful saddler is usually too busy to create good-quality handmade saddles for sale in their shop. Instead saddlery retail outlets offer a large range of goods for sale, repair, cleaning, servicing and fitting and advice on appropriate equipment. Master saddlers in retail will have a workshop on the premises and approved retailers will contract out repairs or servicing.

Your customers will be those people, mainly in rural areas, who ride regularly for a hobby or for stables.

- **How many saddlers are there?** It is hard to estimate the exact number of saddlers, but there are 3116 saddlers and related retailers in the UK.

- **Job prospects and pay** There is fierce competition from other saddlers, tack shops and mail order companies. If you set up your own craft saddlery workshop you need to be professional in your ability and business management in order to survive. You can build up your business by creating good relationships with local riding establishments, stables, racecourses, gymkhanas show event organisers and activity centres. You can also offer a mail order service to increase business. You can earn from £70 up to £200 per week when experienced.

- **Start-up costs** Your major expense will be renting or buying premises with sufficient storage and display space. You need to buy saddle horses to display equipment. These are mock horses costing from £20-£40. You need to spend from £300-£1500 to buy ready-made stock. A range of basic tools and equipment should cost around £5000.

- **How old must you be?** You need to be 16 or over.

- **Training** If you have no previous training you can train by becoming an apprentice to a Master Saddler. The Indenture papers are registered with *The Society of Master Saddlers*. You might find it difficult to find a master saddler who is willing to take an apprentice. An apprenticeship lasts for four years and at the end you will receive a Completion Certificate. The master may wish to send you on courses at one of the institutions mentioned below during this time. This is usually an option for school leavers. Send a £3.00 postal order only to *The Society of Master Saddlers* for the names and addresses of master saddler members and then write for interviews. Training courses in saddlery are run by *The Cordwainers College, The Walsall College of Arts & Technology, and The Rural Development Commission*. There are two private institutions; the *Cambridge & District Saddlery Courses* and *Cumbria School of Saddlery*.

- **Qualifications** You do not need any qualifications to become an apprentice, but during that time you will be expected to pass two specified level II courses of the Saddlery Skills Assessment Scheme so that you can become a Registered Trainee saddler with *The Society of Master Saddlers*. If you have no apprenticeship training you will need to obtain City & Guilds qualifications at one of the institutions named above. These are available at three levels of competence.

Contacts: *The Society of Master Saddlers*, Kettles Farm, Mickfield, Stowmarket, Suffolk IP14 6BY. Tel/fax: 01449-711642; *The Cordwainers College*, Mare Street, Hackney, London E8 3RE. Tel: 020-8985 0273; *The Walsall College of Arts & Technology*, Leather Department, Shelley Campus, Scarborough Road, Walsall, West Midlands WS2 2TY. Tel: 01922-720889; *The Rural Development Commission*, 141 Castle Street, Salisbury, Wilts SP1 3TP. Tel: 01722-336255; *Cambridge & District Saddlery Courses*, 31 St John Street, Bury St Edmunds, Suffolk IP33 1SN. Tel: 01284-700640; *Cumbria School of Saddlery*, Redhills Business Park, Penrith, Cumbria CA11 0DL. Tel: 01768-899919.

See also: Bookbinder.
Find out about: Glove maker.

Sculptor £ – £ £ £ £ £

A sculptor might produce anything from the gigantic 'Angel of the North' to a small clay model for a house. Sculptors use the traditional clay and marble, but also nowadays any kind of material that can be welded together or turned into a free-standing art object.

Traditional sculptors might make clay models that are cast in bronze or carve marble statues for large houses, parks or public buildings. The sculptures can be traditional or modern and of any size.

You will enjoy sculpture if you like feeling materials in your hands and bringing out their hidden qualities. Many traditional sculptors talk about setting free designs that they think are already hidden in the materials.

- **How many sculptors are there?** There are few famous living sculptors in the UK but many more who work unknown.

- **Job prospects and pay** The pay is what you can charge people to pay and this depends like much of art on what is fashionable. If you are employed by a council to produce a public work you might get thousands of pounds.

- **Start-up costs** These will depend on what kind of sculptor you want to be - a non traditional one might require welding tools and blow torches instead of marble blocks and chisels. However, you will certainly need to hire studio space and then buy the tools and materials of your chosen type of sculpture.

- **How old must you be?** Any age.

- **Training** You can teach yourself, go to adult education classes, go to art school or learn through the *Open College of the Arts*. Art school is the traditional route. You might be lucky to find a practising sculptor who will give you private lessons.

- **Qualifications** None needed, but art school degrees are common.

Contacts: Contact your local art schools and adult education colleges.

Shepherd   £ £ £ – £ £ £ £

The hills are green, the sheep are white, the sun is shining. You are standing with your crook in your hand and your sheep dog is sitting by your side. If this is the picture you have of the life you'd like to lead then a shepherd's life might be the one for you.

But this is not a job for anyone who likes an early night or no change in the weather. Looking after sheep requires an unsentimental outlook and a vigorous health. Shepherds are responsible for a flock of sheep and need to know about lambing, dipping, shearing, safe medicine, administration, handling and much more. However, you are likely to be involved in other areas of farm work too as farmers try to keep costs down. You might be employed full-time on an estate. Owning your own flock might prove too expensive. You are more likely to work part-time or be self-employed. On a large estate the top job might involve managing a large flock and several staff. But there is no higher level to go to after that.

• How many shepherds are there? There are 80,000 wool producers in the UK, of which about half will employ one or more shepherds, but there are no exact figures.

• Job prospects and pay Job prospects are poor as flocks increase in size and fewer shepherds are employed. The pay varies from £11,000-13,000 per year for a full-time shepherd and there may be other benefits such as a tied cottage, farm vehicle and dog food. Some shepherds on large estates with more responsibility might earn about £15,000 per year.

• Start-up costs None except your dog and crook if you are employed by a farmer. If you are establishing your own flock then start-up costs will be quite high. You will need to pay for renting or owning pasture and the cost of ewes. You might need buildings for indoor lambing and hay or silage for winter feeding.

• How old must you be? Experience is the most important qualification for a shepherd, hence there are no formal age restrictions. You can be a shepherd from school age to retirement. But if you want to go to Agricultural College you must be 16 or over.

• Training You do need basic training. You can get this on the job, but nowadays you will usually need more. You can take short courses in lambing, shearing, etc, or there are NVQs and National diploma courses of one or two years.

• Qualifications You do not need qualifications, but if you have any formal training you will be at an advantage when seeking work.

Contacts: Your local Agricultural College; *National Sheep Association*, The Sheep Centre, Malvern, Worcester WR13 6PH. Tel: 01684-892661. Fax: 01684-892663.

See also: Gamekeeper, zoo worker, forest worker, dry stone waller.
Find out about: Farmer.

Ship's photographer   £ – £ £ £

Working on board ship while visiting sunny foreign countries sounds a great idea doesn't it? One way you can do this is by becoming a ship's photographer.

Your job would be to take photographs of the passengers, get them printed and then display them for sale. You would attend special events such as dances and take photographs of the participants. You take candid photos and posed shots. The photos are then put on display, usually the next day, and are available for the passengers to buy. You might also take photos at specially arranged sittings by request.

You need to be friendly and efficient. You should be a competent photographer although you will be given basic training. There are also opportunities for photo lab technicians for processing and printing films.

• **Job prospects and pay** Much of the work is seasonal, but some of the larger cruise ship's employ ships photographers all the year round.

• **Start-up costs** Your equipment will be supplied.

• **How old must you be?** 18.

• **Training** It helps to know about photography, but sometimes you will be given the basic training you need on board. For specialist jobs you might need some training in general photography.

• **Qualifications** No specific qualifications are required.

Contacts: Watch the small ads in newspapers and magazines, especially magazines like *Private Eye*. Contact shipping companies directly.

See also: Industrial photographer.
Find out about: picture researcher, ship board entertainer.

Sign language interpreter   £ £ £ – £ £ £ £

If you have ever tried to have a conversation with a deaf person you will know how frustrating it can be for both people if you do not understand their language. Think how they must feel trying to communicate with the officialdom that most people take for granted. As a sign language interpreter you would truly be a deaf person's window on the world.

British Sign Language (BSL) is a fully functional language where a distinctive grammar using handshapes, facial expressions, gestures and body language conveys meaning. It is used by over 70,000 profoundly deaf people for whom English may be a second or third language.

There are few qualified interpreters of sign language in the UK, but they perform a valuable job. Deaf people often find it difficult to communicate with the world at large and an interpreter can be a valuable friend.

You would interpret for deaf people in any number of important situations such as in a court of law, in a doctor's surgery or hospital, in schools or colleges, to the local Council and so on. Your interpretation of your clients' language might be the only way they have of making their true thoughts and feelings known in a difficult situation. You would play a valuable part in their daily lives too as you interpreted for theatre, conferences, news on television and in the workplace.

Sign language interpretation requires a good understanding of the ethics involved in being the source of communication for others.

● **How many sign language interpreters are there?** There are only about 200 registered sign language interpreters in England, Wales and Northern Ireland.

● **Job prospects and pay** As more local authorities realise the need to provide access to information for deaf people the job prospects for sign language interpreters are growing. Where interpreters have been established more posts seem to become available. Pay in Scotland is from about £14,500 for a trainee to about £18,500 for someone with overall responsibility for developing the service. Salaries are probably higher in England. There are opportunities for full-time or part-time, employed or self-employed, or for job sharing.

● **Start-up costs** If you are self-employed you will need to pay for general office equipment and a car will be vital.

● **How old must you be?** As a certain maturity is essential you are unlikely to get work under the age of 21. But the earlier you learn sign language the easier it will be.

● **Training** If you have no sign language skills and want to become a sign language interpreter expect to train for from five to seven years before reaching a level where you can be placed on the Register. You can learn sign language skills at evening classes and then go on to take a qualification. Alternatively you can train at a university.

● **Qualifications** To train as a sign language interpreter you must first obtain a Sign Language qualification - these range from beginners Stage 1 to Interpreter level. In England the register and Examining body the is *Council for the Advancement of Communication with Deaf People (CACDP)* which awards NVQs and is considering registration at level 4. You must hold a Sign Language qualification first. In Scotland the routes are more varied including training at *Heriot-Watt* after you have acquired a qualification in sign language. The *Scottish Association of Sign Language Interpreters (SASLI)* award Sign Language interpreting Awards up to level five.

Both CACDP and SASLI have their own supervision and assessment procedures to decide whether someone has reached a level appropriate for registration. *Durham University* now awards a Master's Degree in teaching BSL (British Sign Language).

Contacts: *Council for the Advancement of Communication with Deaf People* (CACDP), Pelaw House, School of Education, Durham DT1 1TA. Tel: 0191-374 3607. Fax: 0191-374 3605. Text & answerphone: 0191-374 3614. E-mail: durham@cacdp.demon.co.uk. Website: **www.cacdp.demon.co.uk**; *Scottish Association of Sign Language Interpreters* (SASLI), 45 York Place, Edinburgh EH1 3HP. Tel: 0131-557 6370. Fax: 0131-557 4110.

See also: Feng Shui consultant, mobility instructor for guide dogs.
Find out about: Health visitor.

Slimming club leader   £ – £ £ £

If you have ever suffered the agonies of trying to lose weight you will know what a valuable service slimming club organisers serve. The camaraderie coupled with positive reinforcement, sensible advice and regular attendance has helped many people to lose weight and more importantly to keep it off.

You will probably have successfully lost weight yourself if you are considering this career. Although it is possible to set up a slimming club of your own you will find it easier and more rewarding to do so under the auspices of one the major slimming club organisations.

As the organiser your job is to provide support and encouragement to people who want to lose weight. The usual format is a weekly group meeting with a weigh-in, nutritional talk and provision of a healthy eating plan. You arrange the venue, take the money, do the weigh-in and give the talks and make yourself available between meetings for members who need extra support.

Two major slimming organisations *Slimming World* and *Weight Watchers*™ have jobs for slimming club leaders or consultants. You do not have to be medically trained.

● **Job prospects and pay** The main slimming organisations have opportunities for leaders/consultants.

● **Start-up costs** If you become a leader with one of the main organisations the company will deal with the start-up costs. If you are starting your own club you need to rent premises and provide scales, literature, etc.

● **How old must you be?** Although you can join a slimming club from 16 you are unlikely to be accepted as a leader until you are 18+.

● **Training** You will be trained by a slimming organisation if you work for them, but if you are starting on your own no training is necessary. However, you should get some training in basic nutrition from adult education classes.

● **Qualifications** There are no specific requirements, but obviously if you have some nutritional training that will help.

Contacts: *Slimming World*, PO Box 55, Alfreton, Derbyshire DE55 4UE; *Weight Watchers*™, Website: **www.weightwatchers.com**.

See also: Reflexologist.
Find out about: Teacher, nurse, nutritionist.

Stained glass artist   £ – £ £ £

A stained glass artist manipulates coloured light in an architectural context. Being a stained glass artist is part design and part craft. You might be involved with the conservation and restoration of stained glass or you might both design and make the stained glass. As a stained glass artist you would be involved in a technical art form; one that is not only part of our heritage in churches and other major buildings, but nowadays can also be seen in offices, banks, hotels, airports and domestic houses.

You might be employed by a studio or you could be self-employed. Although you could teach yourself, this could have dire consequences both to yourself, the customer and the glass, if you have no adequate understanding of the craft. It is important to try to get training with an approved master.

If you are content to earn money by setting up on a small scale to provide custom-made stained glass panels or lampshades then you could train by attending adult education classes or courses such as those run by *Bournemouth Stained Glass*.

● **How many stained glass artists are there?** There could be thousands of stained glass artists if you include the many who are untrained. But the *British Society of Master Glass Painters* has 500 members, of whom 350 earn their living from stained glass. But this is only a fraction of the industry.

● **Job prospects and pay** If you are taken on by a studio or are self-employed after approved training the prospects can be good. But there are far more people wanting to get a job in a stained glass studio than there are jobs available.

● **Start-up costs** If you set up on your own you will need to hire studio space and buy all your equipment.

- **How old must you be?** As much training now takes place in colleges, you will have to satisfy the age criteria for the college you wish to attend.

- **Training** Many colleges provide training in working with stained glass as an integral part of courses such as fine art, design, public art, architectural and community art and education courses. The courses last from one to four years and there are some part-time options. Ask at your local careers office. You can get an HND, BTEC, BA or MA. For small scale work look for adult education or private courses.

- **Qualifications** People can and do set up without training or qualifications, but this is not recommended. As demand for a place in a studio is so high your best option is to get one of the qualifications offered by a college first.

122

Contacts: *British Society of Master Glass Painters.* Look at their website **www.bsmgp.org.uk** for details of colleges that provide relevant courses. You can contact them byE-mail: secretary@bsmgp.org.uk; *Society of Glass Technology*, 20 Hallam Gate Road, Sheffield S10 5BT. Tel: 0114-2663168. Fax: 0114-2665252. E-mail: gt@glass.demon.co.uk. Website: **www.sgt.org** (to encourage and advance the study of the history, art, science, design, manufacture, after treatment, distribution and end use of glass of any kind); *Bournemouth Stained Glass*, Tel: 020-7790 2333. Website: **http//www.hetleys.co.uk**.

See also: Bookbinder, glassblower, china restorer.
Find out about: Artist.

Stone mason   £ – £ £

Stone masons repair and restore stonework on old buildings as well as providing stonework for new buildings. There are two kinds of masons - bankers and fixers. Bankers work in workshops. Stone is delivered to the workshops straight from the quarries and banker masons work from drawings and plans to prepare the rough stone ready for use in a building. They shape it and 'dress' it to give it the surface that the customer wants, e.g. polished, rough or smooth. Sometimes they carve figures or patterns into the stone. Fixer masons work on site and work from plans to assemble the stone where it is needed and make sure it stays level. They fix the stones together with mortar and attach the final stone facing to walls or metal frames.

In large firms these two kinds of masonry work are done by different people. In small, often family firms, a mason may do both types of work.

Masons use traditional tools such as mallets, chisels, trowels, levels and plumb-lines, but also modern power tools.

Some masons specialise as memorial masons who design and cut memorials such as headstones. If you become a memorial mason you might decide to specialise in particular stone such as granite or marble.

The main skill that you need to be a memorial mason is skill in letter carving. You need an interest in history, an eye for design, patience and an awareness of safety.

- **How many stone masons are there?** Anyone can call themselves a stone mason, so the numbers are hard to discover. There are about 3000 memorial masons employed by genuine companies.

- **Job prospects and pay** A qualified craftsman earns about £190 per week. Although there is steady work for stone masons in general, obviously memorial masonry is not an expanding industry! Job prospects are not easy to assess as many masons work until they are very old. If you are determined, you should be able to find work.

- **Start-up costs** Many good memorial masons start in the garage with not much more than their tools. The customer pays a deposit sufficient for the price of the stone. As you progress you will probably want to buy grip blasting equipment. A computer for the administrative work is always necessary nowadays.

- **How old must you be?** As long as you can do the work effectively you can work to any age you like.

- **Training** The masonry industry is unregulated so no training is required. Most young masons train with employers using a programme arranged by the *Construction Industry Training Board (CITB)*. This combines college work with on-the-job training to get NVQs levels 2 and 3. This equals the first part of a traditional apprenticeship. Some Modern Apprenticeships may be available to help you get NVQ level 3. Usually you need four GCSEs for this and you get a wage while you train. You can start a Modern Apprenticeship any time after leaving full-time education, but 16-18 year olds are given priority. However, to be a proper memorial mason you do need training and there is now an NVQ 2, soon an NVQ 3, qualification.

- **Qualifications** There are no formal qualifications, but an NVQ will help teach you the basic skills. You need a good general education with GCSEs and drawing skills.

Contacts: *Stone Federation*, Construction House, 56-64 Leonard Street, London

EC2A 4JX; *National Association of Memorial Masons*, 27a Albert Street, Rugby, Warwickshire CV21 2SG. Tel: 01788-542264. Fax: 01788-542276. E-mail: enquiries@namm.org.uk. Website: **www.namm.org.uk**; *Building Crafts College*, 153 Great Titchfield Street, London W1P 7FR. Tel: 020-7636 0480; *Construction Industry Training Board* (CITB), Careers Advisory Service, Bircham Newton, King's Lynn, Norfolk PE31 6RH. Tel: 01485-577577. For some courses see Website: **www.buildingconservation.com/courses/nvq.html**.

See also: Dry stone waller.
Find out about: Wood carver.

Stunt artist   £ £ £ £ £

Don't be fooled - becoming a stunt artist is *not* an easy job. What seems easy on a television or film screen is the result of years of practice and training and an understanding of safety procedures. You might be asked to do anything from diving off a cliff to driving a motor cycle over an open bridge. You would be standing in for the main actors of the film.

However, if you are fit and active and have some training in sporting skills such as horse riding, fencing, swimming, etc, you might consider this as a career.

You need to have good steady nerves, but not be so blasé that you do not consider all the risks involved and take all the necessary steps to eliminate or reduce them. It *is* a dangerous career and not one for the faint-hearted.

With experience you could co-ordinate stunts for others as well as do them yourself.

● **How many stunt artists are there?** There are about 200 stunt artists.

● **Job prospects and pay** The work is intermittent and seldom full-time. Work for TV is often only for a few days at a time. Film work provides much longer contracts. Stunt artists work as employees but are classed as self-employed for tax purposes. Contact *Equity* (*British Actor's Equity Association*) for details about the recent qualifications and range of skills required to register. You can earn about £300 per day or £1,251 a week. If you arrange stunts your pay will be about £400 per day or £1,590 a week.

● **Start-up costs** The cost of training in sports.

● **How old must you be?** The minimum age is 18 although most people are about 30 when they join the profession. You can go on as long as you are alive. New members are accepted onto the *Equity (British Actor's Equity Association)* stunt register between the ages of 18 and 30.

● **Training** Most training takes place on the job, but sporting skills, driving skills, etc, can be obtained through the relevant local organisations.

● **Qualifications** None specified.

Contacts: *Stunt Co-ordinators Guild*, 'Windrush', 15 Marshall Avenue, Worthing, West Sussex BN14 0ES. Tel/fax: 01903-873105; *Equity (British Actor's Equity Association)*, Guild House, Upper St Martins Lane, London WC2H 9EG. Tel: 020-7379 6000. Fax: 020-7379 7001. E-mail: info@equity.org.uk. Website: **www.equity.org.uk**.

See also: Hot air balloonist, racing driver, jockey, courier, deep sea diver, explorer, mountain guide.
Find out about: Police officer.

Tai Chi teacher   £ £

You may have seen a film of Chinese people practising Tai Chi in their parks. Everyone does it from the very young to the very old. Slow controlled movements of the whole body are not as easy as they look. They exercise every part of you in a systematic way. This ancient martial art makes you supple and increases stamina and good health. It also concentrates your mind. In the UK it is becoming very popular with people who want the discipline of martial arts training without the fighting element. In fact Tai Chi practitioners are usually very gentle people with a peaceful outlook on life.
    You can work full-time (perhaps 12-20 hours a week) or part-time.

● **How many Tai Chi teachers are there?** There are about 200 instructors in the UK.

● **Job prospects and pay** Probably not more then 50 instructors make a full-time living from Tai Chi. Most have a second job. For example, one instructor also runs alternative health exhibitions, produces magazines and runs a mail-order business. A few Tai Chi instructors have international reputations and can therefore earn money by travelling widely to teach. The average pay is from £15-25 an hour.

● **Start-up costs** You need to hire a hall and produce and distribute posters.

● **How old must you be?** As long as you are fit and healthy you can teach Tai Chi into your seventies.

- **Training** To be a Tai Chi teacher you must train for many years. You do not have to go to China, but you need to find a teacher in the UK who is properly qualified. Traditionally you find a reputable instructor prepared to teach you and then acquire and develop your skills over many years. Beware of a number of Tai Chi 'instructor's courses' run by one or two people not recognised by any of the Tai Chi authorities.

- **Qualifications** At present you do not need any qualifications although more local and national sport and health authorities are asking for proof of expertise. The *Tai Chi Union for Great Britain (TCUGB)* has started a pilot scheme of three levels for certification.

Contacts: *The Tai Chi Union for Great Britain*, 69 Kilpatrick Gardens, Clarkston, Glasgow G76 7RF. Tel: 0141-638 2946. Fax: 0141-621 1220. E-mail: taichi@dial.pipex.com. Website: **www.dialspace.dial.pipex.com/taichi**.

See also: Reflexologist, chiropractor.
Find out about: Sports teacher.

Taxidermist   £ £ £ £ £

If you have a strong stomach, love animals and are good with your hands then consider a career in taxidermy. This is the art and craft of stuffing animals and birds so that they not only look lifelike but are also preserved. You can immediately see the difference between good and bad taxidermy in museums. Compare the mangy unnatural creatures with the lifelike and well-preserved examples. It can be a satisfying career and of benefit to science.

Taxidermy is not for the morbid; you will have a love of nature and a general aptitude for using your hands.

You might choose to specialise in creatures killed in road accidents or game species. Whichever animals or birds you choose to work with you must keep clear details of how you obtained the creatures and make sure that you understand the legal aspects of obtaining the bodies for taxidermy. This can be complicated so consult experts and books.

You will be at little risk from disease because specimens wrapped in polythene will keep well in a deep freeze for several months without deterioration. You must follow the usual precautions of washing hands and work surfaces. Only rats and similar creatures should perhaps be avoided as they can harbour a lethal disease.

The main work, apart from commercial work, is in museums where you might prepare specimens for scientific collections, give advice and undertake surveys in areas of natural history conservation, or carry out a wide range of additional duties.

ACTUALLY THAT'S **NOT** THE WAY I REMEMBER HAMMY

● **How many taxidermists are there?** There are about 150 taxidermists who belong to *The Guild of Taxidermists* and approximately 400 unregistered amateurs in the UK. Of these, no more than 12 are employed in local government museums.

● **Job prospects and pay** There are no large taxidermy firms in the UK so if you want to work in a commercial environment you are more likely to be self-employed. However, there are opportunities in museums - national, museum area services and local government museums. But be warned that there has been no increase in available jobs over the past ten years, and some museum taxidermy sections have closed. So job prospects in the museum sector are not good. If you work in a national museum your salary could reach as much as £25,000 a year. If you become self-employed then you will need to charge as much as any other skilled craftsperson.

● **Start-up costs** Catalogues from taxidermy supply firms will give you an idea of prices for equipment and materials (see addresses below).

● **How old must you be?** There are no formal age limits for becoming a taxidermist.

● **Training** There are no institutional training courses, but you may occasionally find one or two day courses advertised by individual taxidermists. These are more likely to be of interest to you if you only want to practise taxidermy as a hobby.

The best option is to find a commercial taxidermist prepared to teach you, or to learn on the job in a museum (for which you need higher qualifications). This is usually difficult so you need to learn from books and legally obtain a specimen to practise on. Look in your library for relevant books such as *Taxidermy - A Complete Manual* by John Metcalf. Joining *The Guild of Taxidermists* will give you access to advice and information.

● **Qualifications** There are no formal qualifications for a career in taxidermy, but general skills include manual dexterity, artistic talent, a familiarity and interest in living creatures and a desire to be active in field work. If you want to work in museums you will need to be qualified in maths, English, biology or chemistry. If you want to set up as a commercial taxidermist you must register with the *Department of the Environment, Transport and the Regions* and follow their system for obtaining specimens.

It is best to get as high a level of qualifications as you can for your own benefit, that of your customers and in case you later decide to change career.

Contacts: *The Guild of Taxidermists*, Kelvingrove, Glasgow G3 8AG. Tel: 0141-287 2671. Fax: 0141-287 2690; *Department of the Environment*, Wildlife Division, Tollgate House, Houlton Street, Bristol BS2 9DJ; *Nature Conservancy Council*, Northminster House, Peterborough, PE1 1UA; *Lorne Taxidermy Supplies*, Kilnhillock Cottages, By Cullen, Buckie, Banffshire AB56 2TB. Tel: 01542-840 176; *Eyedentitiy Products*, The Manor House, Church Hill, Saxmundham, Suffolk IP17 1EU. Tel: 01728-603171. Fax: 01728-603101; *Snowdonia Taxidermy Studios*, Llanrust, North Wales LL26. Tel: 01492-640 664; *Department of the Environment*, Transport and the Regions, Eland House, Bressenden Place, London SW1E 5DU. Tel: 020-7890 3000. Website: **www.detr.gov.uk**.

See also: Embalmer.
Find out about: Museum worker.

Teacher of English as a foreign language   £ £ £

Up to one quarter of the world's population – and this number is increasing – require assistance from a teacher of English as a foreign language. It is estimated that by the year 2000 over one billion people will be learning English - and they need somebody like you to teach them.

A TEFL (Teacher of English as a Foreign Language) qualification has long been a popular passport to working abroad or working in language schools in Britain. Students in particular use it as a stepping stone to work during a GAP year or post graduation while waiting for other work. But it can also be a fulfilling career in itself.

As a TEFL teacher you would give regular classes to foreign language students who want to master the English language at any level from complete beginner to advanced.

● **How many TEFL teachers are there?** The *British Council* employs about 300 but there are many more.

● **Job prospects and pay** Job prospects are good both in the UK and abroad. You are most likely to gain employment in a private language school.

However, once you have experience, the *British Council* recruits about 300 English teachers for its world-wide network of teaching centres. For this you need a degree, a diploma level TEFL or PGCE in TEFL and a minimum of two years overseas experience. The terms and conditions are excellent.

● **Start-up costs** Your only start-up cost is your tuition. A course costs from £400 to £1000 depending on the course and institution. See the British Council website below (contacts) for a list of institutions that provide TEFL/TESOL courses.

● **How old must you be?** The usual minimum age is 20 although some courses accept people aged 18.

● **Training** TEFL (Teaching English as a Foreign Language) and TESOL (Teaching English to Speakers of Other Languages) essentially mean the same thing. You don't need any previous experience, but you do need a good standard of education. Often this is a first degree, but with two good A levels you can sometimes enter the profession by taking a certificate qualification. It is also possible to learn TEFL by distance learning.

● **Qualifications** The most commonly accepted qualifications are the Cambridge/RSA and Trinity College London Certificate or state Qualified Teacher Status (QTS). But note that many TEFL/TESOL courses do not confer QTS. That means that although you might be able to teach in private language schools in the UK and abroad you will not be able to teach in a UK state school without the relevant qualification.

Contacts: The British Council website **www.britcoun.org/english/index.htm** gives a full list of institutions providing TEFL/TESOL courses.

See also: Sign language interpreter, tour guide.
Find out about: Teacher, youth club leader.

A cottage with a thatched roof and roses around the door is one of the abiding if misleading pictures people have of the British countryside. However, there are still many buildings with thatched roofs which need regular maintenance and occasional re-roofing. One of the most interesting thatching jobs of recent years has been the thatching of the rebuilt Globe Theatre in Southwark.

Thatchers use traditional tools and, depending on the requirements of the building, one of three types of thatching material - Long Straw, Combed Wheat Straw or Water Reed (Norfolk Reed). You need to gain experience with all three types of material because the techniques for thatching with them vary depending on which type you use. If you do your work well it will last for between 15 to 60 years, depending on which material is used. On a typical thatched roof the ridge will need restructuring every 20 years or so. The thatch is applied directly to the rafters. A common fear is that thatch harbours pests, but the thickness of a thatched roof deters them. Wire netting is sometimes added to prevent infestation.

A master thatcher working alone can normally finish thatching a 1000 square foot roof in three to four weeks.

Your work will be dependent on the weather - it is no good trying to thatch a roof in a high wind or pouring rain. You need to enjoy working out of doors and you need to have a good head for heights!

- **How many thatchers are there?** Nobody knows, especially as there are many semiskilled workers who are not strictly competent thatchers. The National Society of Master Thatchers has about 72 members.

- **Job prospects and pay** There are still about 55,000 thatched houses in the UK so the job is still in demand. The rates you can charge depend on the materials, structure and roof size. As a guide you can earn about £60-70 per week as an apprentice.

- **Start-up costs** You need basic thatching tools.

- **How old must you be?** You can start as a young apprentice at 16.

- **Training** The best training you can get is to become apprenticed to a master thatcher and learn on the job. Apprentices train for four to five years. Your apprenticeship might be supervised by a local government officer or the *Rural Development Commission (RDC)*. You can get a list of master thatchers from the *National Society of Master Thatchers*. However, the *RDC* also provides short courses to supplement training.

• **Qualifications** No formal qualifications are necessary, but to become eligible for inclusion in the *National Society of Master Thatchers* you need to have reached the required standard.

Contacts: *National Society of Master Thatchers*, 20 The Laurels, Tetsworth, Thame, Oxfordshire OX9 7BH. Tel/fax: 01844-281568; *Rural Development Commission*, Training and Productivity Section, 141 Castle Street, Salisbury, Wiltshire SP1 3TP Tel: 01722-336255. Fax: 01722-332769.

See also: Dry stone waller, forest officer.
Find out about: Roofer, builder.

Tour guide

£ £ £ £ – £ £ £ £ £

If you like meeting people and love telling people about your part of the world, becoming a tour guide is probably your ideal job. To be a tour guide you need a specialist knowledge of one area and to be able to provide a service for visitors. Some tour guides work on coach tours and similar expeditions. A tour guide is the lynch pin of any good tour.

You might take people around tourist attractions, work in one important building such as a cathedral or stately home, or travel on coaches in the UK or abroad to explain the attractions and keep a general eye on people. Tour guides are also now employed in a variety of unusual places such as disued coal mines.

Tourist Board Registered Blue Badge Guides have been selected, trained, examined and registered by a Tourist Board.

• **Job prospects and pay** The work is freelance and seasonal and your pay depends on who employs you. In some cases you might also receive tips. A London Blue Badge guide can earn about £110+ per day.

• **Start-up costs** Usually none.

• **How old must you be** Normally 18 or over.

• **Training** You can train with Tourist Boards and local tourism authorities and the courses are usually part-time. There are also some private agencies. Once in a job you can work towards an NVQ in Travel Services (Commentaries and Interpretation for Tourism).

• **Qualifications** You need good conversational skills and a knowledge of one or two foreign languages is useful and for some jobs perhaps essential. Your personal qualities are more important than your academic qualifications in this job, but some employers will ask for GCSEs or higher. Tourist Board Registered Guides are entitled to wear the professional Blue Badge.

Contacts: *The Travel Training Company*, The Cornerstone, The Broadway, Woking, Surrey GU21 5AR. Tel: 01403-727321. Fax: 01483-756698. E-mail: sales@tttc.co.uk. Website: **www.tttc.co.uk** (send a large SAE and a cheque for £3 for their careers pack); *Institute of Travel and Tourism*, 113 Victoria Street, St Albans, Herts AL1 3JT Tel: 01727-854395; *British Tourist Authority* (BTA), Website: **www.visitbritain.com.**

See also: Comedian, TEFL teacher.
Find out about: Receptionist.

Trichologist

£ £ – £ £ £

Not everyone who likes working with hair becomes a hairdresser. Trichology is a related career that requires a more fundamental understanding of hair. A trichologist diagnoses hair and scalp conditions and prescribes treatment. Your clients will come to you with problems such as thinning hair, scalp disorders or even with healthy hair for advice about the best way to look after it. In this job you use massage, heat and electrical treatments and lotions and ointments to treat clients' hair problems. You also advise on diet and hair care.

Although most trichologists work in private clinics many of these are attached to hairdressers' salons. Indeed many hairdressers train as trichologists to add another skill to their services. Clients either arrange an appointment directly or are referred to you by their doctor or hairdresser.

Private practice is not the only work. There may also be opportunities to work in science research, cosmetic firms or in the pharmaceutical industry as a consultant in product development.

You need to be interested in science, practical, sympathetic and have a good business sense. You should also be tactful - people do get embarrassed if their hairline is receding, for example!

● **How many trichologists are there?** There are about 250 qualified trichologists in the UK. But there are also unqualified trichologists working.

● **Job prospects and pay** Job prospects are good; you can earn at least £10,000 per year.

● **Start-up costs** You need the cost of business premises and equipment if you start your own private practice.

● **How old must you be?** To train at the *Institute of Trichologists* you must be 18+. Apart from that you can start at any age.

● **Training** The *Institute of Trichologists* has exams at three levels and these can be studied for part-time, by distance learning or at day or evening classes. You then enter the profession by training with a qualified trichologist.

● **Qualifications** There is no law that you have to be qualified to be a trichologist, but clearly your clients will have more confidence in you if you are qualified.

Contacts: *Institute of Trichologists*, PO Box 142, Stevenage, SG1 5UX. Tel: 01483-387182. E-mail: trichologists@ambernet.co.uk.

See also: Alternative medicine practitioner, wig-maker.
Find out about: Hairdresser.

Typographer £ £ £

Typography is the art or style of printing or using type effectively and creatively. Type has to be designed and set on the page so that it is not only easy to read but looks good to the eye. The fact that computers have replaced metal type has not reduced the need for the work of typographers. It is not only books that have a typographic aspect - advertisements, brochures, posters, packaging - anything which uses the written word needs a typographer.

The work involves not just the ease with which the words can be read, but also the costs, print methods and the style of the lettering and the page area of print as a whole.

You need to have a good command of English, a keen eye for slight differences and an artistic view of the printed word. As most of the work now involves computer design systems you also need to be computer literate.

● **How many typographers are there?** The *Society of Typographic Designers* has 733 members, but not all of them would class themselves as typographers.

● **Job prospects and pay** Most students join a design consultancy straight out of college. After three or four years many of them move into freelancing or teaching.

● **Start-up costs** None.

● **How old must you be?** Normally 18 to start a college course.

● **Training** There is none laid down, but naturally a full-time course at an accredited college should give you a good foundation.

● **Qualifications** Some typographers have no qualifications, but an HND or degree is desirable. To become a member of the *Society of Typographic Designers* you must give the Council of the Society evidence of your competence.

Contacts: Contact your local colleges for information on courses with a design or typographic input. *Society of Typographic Designers*, Chapelfield Cottage, Randwick, Stroud, Glos GL6 6HS. Tel: 01453-759311.

See also: Calligrapher, bookbinder.
Find out about: Printer, copywriter.

Undertaker/funeral director £ £ – £ £ £ £

Undertakers are now more usually known as funeral directors. The work involves collecting and preparing bodies for burial or cremation, checking the legal requirements are complied with, storing the bodies until the funeral, making all the funeral arrangements and then conveying bodies to funerals and remaining in attendance. This is not as macabre a job as it sounds and much of the work requires meeting people and lifting and carrying.

Your job starts before the funeral when you are contacted by friends and relatives of the deceased and need to make sure the relevant papers are in order. You need to be sympathetic and tactful because you will be on hand 24 hours a day to deal with stressed relatives.

Before the funeral you need to arrange visits to the chapel of rest, complete forms, estimate costs, deal with the clergy and all the extras such as obituaries in the press, service sheets and so on. You arrange for the hearse and cortege and attend the funeral.

You do not need to be Christian but you do need to understand church ritual. You will be dealing with people from all religions.

You can work full-time or part-time and some freelance work is available. Self-employed workers in the business tend to be embalmers.

How many undertakers are there? There are 3500 funeral directors in the UK. About 800 of these belong to the *Co-op* societies and 550 belong to *Service Corporation International*. The total number of jobs of all kinds in funeral services in the UK is about 16,000.

Job prospects and pay The number of staff depends on the size of the company. A small company may have only one or two full-time staff and call on many freelancers who help out and drive cars when needed. Many firms are small family businesses and it can be hard to join these without family connections. But this is changing and there are now a number of larger firms.

Start-up costs If you want to start a new business from scratch the start-up costs can be high because you will need a lot of capital for premises and vehicles. This is especially so if you want the business to have its own mortuary and embalming facilities. The only laws that apply are the normal health and safety regulations.

How old must you be? There are no age restrictions, but you must be fit and able to lift and carry. However, there are roles that do not require any manual labour.

Training You do not need any training, but there are many training schemes available.

Qualifications None - but qualifications are available. The *National Association of Funeral Directors* runs a part-time modular Diploma in Funeral Directing. There is also a BTEC in Funeral Directing.

Contacts: *The Society of Allied & Independent Funeral Directors* (SAIF), Crowndale House, 1 Ferdinand Place, Camden, London NW1 8EE. Tel: 020-7267 6777. Fax: 020-7267 1147. E-mail: info@saif.org.uk. Website: **http://www.saif.org.uk**; *The National Association of Funeral Directors*, 618 Warwick Road, Solihull, West Midlands B91 1AA. Tel: 0121-7111343. Fax: 0121-7111351.
Website: **www.home.netcentral.co.uk/boulton/n_a_f_d.htm**.

See also: Embalmer, butler, housekeeper.
Find out about: Social worker.

If you are a committed vegetarian and your cooking skills are excellent, why not become a vegetarian caterer? You could cater for private parties, directors' dinners, weddings, lunch time workers - the list is endless.

More and more people are becoming vegetarians and there are many who find catering difficult because they cannot think beyond a nut cutlet. Vegetarian food can be exciting and tasty and you would be catering for people who would not only appreciate your cooking skills but your skill in preparing a fully vegetarian menu as well. There are vegetarian restaurants and even accommodation where being a vegetarian is part of the rules.

You need to ensure that your premises are suitable for food preparation and conform to the correct health and safety standards. The relevant department at your local council can advise you about this. It might mean that you have to invest in new equipment or the preparation of surfaces, but this will be part of your initial investment.

Publicity will come high on your list of initial requirements, but once you become known you will find that you get as much work as you need by word of mouth. Start by leafleting your local area, speak to your local newspapers, tell everyone you meet of your new venture.

● **Job prospects and pay** Price your food and services to reflect the realistic costs of your ingredients, time, travel, etc. Compare your prices with local non-vegetarian caterers to get an idea of prices. You can undercut them a bit because they have to include the expense of meat, but do not make yourself so cheap that you lose respect. The job prospects will be what you make of them. You can start by working part-time, perhaps in the evenings only, then, when business picks up, turn full-time.

● **Start-up costs** These will depend on how much kitchen equipment you need to buy and the cost of any changes required to meet health and safety rules.

● **How old must you be?** There is no age limit, but common sense suggests that anyone under the age of 18 will not have the necessary experience.

● **Training** You can teach yourself, learn at adult education classes or attend courses at cookery schools. Try your meals out on family and friends first and practise until you can cook the same food over and again without a hitch. Practise cooking in your friends' homes too in case you are asked to use customers' own ovens. Some colleges let you specialise in vegetarian cookery and *The Vegetarian Society* offers a Cordon Vert Diploma Course for which you have to attend four one week intensive modules.

● **Qualifications** You do not need any qualifications, but obviously customers will be impressed if you hold a relevant award from a recognised institution.

Contacts: Your local adult education centre or college for information about cookery courses. *The Vegetarian Society of the UK Ltd*, Parkdale, Dunham Road, Altrincham, Cheshire WA14 4QG. Tel: 0161-928 0793. E-mail: info@vegsoc.org.
Website: **www.vegsoc.uk** The Vegetarian Society website also has a list of other colleges that run courses in vegetarian cookery or catering as well as useful books and the addresses of relevant organisations.
organisations.

See also: Housekeeper, butler, party planner, Cordon Bleu chef.
Find out about: Cookery writer.

Wallpaper designer   £ £ £

Wallpaper has never gone out of fashion in spite of the recent habit of paint coverings for walls. Wallpaper comes in a multitude of designs, colours and textures and is popular for decoration from the mansions of the rich to the smallest flat.

But each roll of wallpaper has to be designed by someone and that someone could be you. It is not just a question of making one pattern to be repeated. That pattern has to fit not only with itself on one roll but link with the patterns of other rolls. This is why you often lose a certain amount of wallpaper when hanging it, because you have to adjust it upwards or downwards to fit the pattern correctly.

Designers in wallpaper companies work as part of a team and the results are produced to be sold up and down the country. However, you can also work from home.

● **How many wallpaper designers are there?** The wallpaper industry estimates that the numbers are in hundreds rather than in thousands.

● **Job prospects and pay** The job market is very competitive with many more college leavers applying for posts than there are jobs available. Once you are employed as a wallpaper designer you can expect to start on £12,000. Most of the posts are full-time with part-time an option depending on the company and personal circumstances.

- **Start-up costs** You can easily work from home and be self-employed. Start-up costs are minimal with talent being the major resource required.

- **How old must you be?** Any age restrictions are those laid down by the entrance requirements of colleges.

- **Training** Once employed your training would consist of working alongside a senior Stylist.

- **Qualifications** You will usually need an HND or BA in surface pattern.

Contacts: Contact colleges with relevant courses for prospectuses and admissions requirements.

See also: Stained glass window artist, typographer, calligrapher.
Find out about: Artist.

Wardrobe master/mistress

The wardrobe master or mistress looks after the costumes for theatres, film studios, television studios and other venues where shows are put on.

The job entails ensuring that clothes are bought, made, borrowed or adapted for a production and that the relevant costume fits the relevant actor or actress. In repertory theatre the job also involves looking after the costume store. The work can be very stressful because of the performance deadlines. Each costume must be cleaned and repaired as necessary and stored safely. You would also be in charge of ensuring that if the production moves the costumes are transported safely and arrive on time. Whether male or female you will need to know how to sew a costume, do repairs to it, and be imaginative in creating new costumes. You need to be able to translate drawings into costumes. You need a good knowledge of materials. Your work might also involve hiring costumes and accessories rather than buying them.

You might have a number of wardrobe assistants in your charge to help you with routine sewing, ironing and cleaning of costumes. You would also supervise dressers who dress artists for their performances, look after wigs and generally assist the actors. Some wardrobe assistants work as dressers.

You are likely to be employed in theatre, film or television industries as a theatrical costumier.

AND THIS IS YOUR MAGIC CARPET

- **How many wardrobe masters/mistresses are there?** Nobody knows.

- **Job prospects and pay** There are only a limited number of posts so job prospects will require persistence and will depend upon being in the right place at the right time. Start as a dresser or wardrobe assistant to gain experience. Work your way up to wardrobe master/mistress. When you have trained your pay will be about £10,000, but salaries vary between companies and will increase as you become more experienced.

- **Start-up costs** None.

- **How old must you be?** Normally at least 18.

- **Training** The best training is experience, so volunteer to help with amateur productions. However, you can get City and Guilds and BTEC National, Higher National and degrees in costuming. There are also some specialist courses such as the one run by Bristol Old Vic.

- **Qualifications** None are needed, but a qualification in costume design, costuming and/or history would be helpful. As with most jobs you need a good general education at GCSE level.

Contacts: Ask in your local library for the addresses of local theatre companies and offer your services for free to learn your trade. You can then approach larger companies for the possibility of paid work. You can find jobs advertised in *The Stage and Television Today*. Bristol Old Vic Theatre School, 2 Downside Road, Clifton, Bristol BS8 2XF. Tel: 0117-973 3535. Fax: 0117-923 9371. Website: **www.oldvic.drama.ac.uk/wardrobe.html**.

See also: Embroiderer, wigmaker.
Find out about: dressmaker, tailor.

Waste paper merchant

Collecting and selling waste paper is a popular money-making activity by many local charities. If you want to make a living from it, you need to work on a larger scale. The modern enthusiasm for recycling means that many companies and other organisations want to dispose of waste paper and some are even prepared to pay you to take it away.

Waste paper is now a large part of the basic material used in paper mills and the mills prefer to buy British waste. There are 97 pulp, paper and board mills in the UK and 63 per cent of the paper and board they produce is created with waste paper pulp.

You need to arrange to collect waste paper on a regular basis from companies, homes, shops and other places where it is produced in excess as rubbish. You then need a place to store it and a means of transporting it to where it will be bought.

You need to have a van and somewhere to store the paper before selling it on to paper mills. Occasionally councils will buy waste paper and resell it to paper mills.

● How many waste paper merchants are there? Councils and some small organisations act as their own waste paper merchants. The number of full-time independent contractors is probably quite small.

● Job prospects and pay? Your profits on the paper itself will depend on the going rate which fluctuates according to demand for the finished product. You must be prepared to store large amounts of paper until the industry is prepared to pay for it. You can charge some companies for removing waste paper. Your job prospects will depend on how well you advertise and promote your business.

● Start-up costs You can start with one van and a garage, but eventually you will need more vans or a lorry and warehousing for storage.

● How old must you be? 17+.

● Training You don't need any training, but it will help you to work with an established merchant to see how the business is run.

● Qualifications None.

Contacts: *Paper Education and Training Council*, Papermakers House, Rivenhall Road, Westlea, Swindon, Wiltshire SN5 7BD. Website: **www.paper.org.uk**; *Waste Management Industry Training and Advisory Board* (WAMITAB), PO Box 176, Northampton NN1 1SB. Tel: 01604-231950; *Institute of Wastes Management*, 9 Saxon Court, St Peter's Gardens, Northampton NN1 1SX. Tel: 01604-620426; *Environmental Services*

Association, 154 Buckingham Palace road, London SW1W 9TR. Tel: 020-7824 8882. Fax: 020-7824 8753.

See also: Pest control officer.
Find out about: Environmental health officer.

Water dowser (water diviner)   £ – ££

The words water dowser or water diviner conjure up a picture of an old man with a forked twig in his hands walking over a field. It has an air of magic about it - after all who can find water just by watching a twig twitch?

But water dowsers are now serious business people with clients among farmers, oil companies and others who need an accurate idea of where water lies beneath their land. The term dowser also includes searching out hidden minerals, surveying sites, finding archaeological ruins, tracing hidden objects and testing soils. However, it is water that is most usually associated with the term.

There is no satisfactory explanation for dowsing so you need to believe in it. It is associated with brain rhythms and muscular responses and most dowsers use an instrument such as a rod, forked twig or pendulum to amplify their responses. You hold the rod or pendulum in your hands or hand and walk over the ground. When you reach water your hands will produce tiny muscular spasms and the rod will twitch or the pendulum will move.

You can be a water dowser or diviner - anyone can. It takes perseverance and practise although some people are naturally gifted at dowsing. The job depends on the time of year and the amount of rain. In drought conditions you will be employed to find new water courses. When there is a lot of rain you will obviously not be needed!

● **How many water dowsers are there?** There are unknown numbers of water dowsers/diviners within the UK. Of those who are members of *The British Society of Dowsers,* there are 14 professionals and six others.

● **Job prospects and pay** The better your track record the better your chances of employment. You manage fees yourself so your pay will be what you can negotiate. Full-time dowsers are rare and there is probably not enough work for a full-time water dowser as the job depends on the amount of rain.

● **Start-up costs** Dowsing equipment normally only costs a few pounds.

- **How old must you be?** There are no age restrictions, but you do need to be able-bodied and mobile.

- **Training** You can practise by yourself, but you would be sensible to attend courses held by *The British Society of Dowsers* or other courses across the country. You need to become proficient and then accumulate a reliable dossier of dowsing work.

- **Qualifications** You do not need any qualifications, but dowsers are only as good as their track records. No dowser is 100 per cent accurate, but good dowsers can be 95-98 per cent accurate.

Contact: *The British Society of Dowsers*, Sycamore barn, Hastingleigh, Ashford, Kent TN25 5HW. Tel/Fax: 01233-750253.

See also: Feng Shui consultant.
Find out about: Geologist.

Web page designer   £ £ £ £ £

With the Internet such big business nowadays and popular with individuals and large companies alike, there is a growing need for people who can make websites stand out from the rest. There are more than 50 million users of the Internet so there is huge scope for talented web page designers. If you are computer literate, at home on the Internet and have excellent design skills, this could be your ideal job.

A web page is the page of information that someone posts on the Internet. It can be simply a page or more of writing or intricate with images, video clips, sound clips and so on. The art comes in providing the information and links to other parts of the site and other sites and yet making the pages easy to use and interesting to look at.

Anyone can create a web page and publish it on the Internet, but not everyone can design a good web page. If you understand computers and the Internet and have good design skills you can earn money from designing web pages for people. Companies in particular want web page designers who can create a web page to suit corporate identities, products and services and who can make their web pages eye-catching and informative.

Web pages must not only look good but work efficiently. You can supplement the designs by offering continuing site management and web advice and support. Your clients can be individuals who want a simple web page but are unsure of their computer skills, or companies who want a major Internet site designed. Your clients will be more likely to be individuals as companies nowadays often employ their own in-house computer experts.

- **How many web-page designers are there?** The Internet is so vast and so many people design pages that there is no way of knowing the numbers.

- **Job prospects and pay** Obviously if you work as an in-house designer for a major company you would get a salary. As a self-employed designer your income and prospects will depend on how many customers you attract and the quality of your work. You can advertise on the Internet of course! As an example of what you can earn, typical charges by independent web page designers are £100 for a single Home page (the main site page) plus £75 per additional page.

- **Start-up costs** Your main cost will be a fast up-to-date computer with appropriate modem and Internet connection. You will probably need a fast line to compete. You also will need the appropriate software.

- **How old must you be?** Any age - computer whiz kids are often teenagers!

- **Training** Computer experts can be self taught, but courses in design skills or advanced computer skills can be useful.

- **Qualifications** None needed, but again qualifications in IT or design would help. For any in-house company post you will need degree level qualifications.

Contacts: Advertise on the Internet - after all, your own web pages will be your best advertisement! Also place ads in trade magazines and general computer magazines.

See also: Computer games designer.
Find out about: Computer technician.

Wheelwright   £ £

A wheelwright makes wooden wheels, but this is a declining craft. Traditionally wheels were made of wood and bound with iron. They were made for carriages, wagons and other wheeled forms of transport before the days of mass production. Nowadays wheelwrights make wheels for individuals with old carriages, horse-trotting carriages and museums. Anyone who wants wooden wheels on a traditional vehicle repaired would contact a wheelwright.

To be a good wheelwright you need the skills of a carpenter and a blacksmith. You might start with a hub fashioned on a lathe from an aged wood such as elm. You use a special tool to open the centre of the hub to place a metal bearing in it and then chisel rectangular holes around the hub to take the spokes. The spokes are carved from a wood such as ash and radiate out from the hub to meet a rim of mortised wooden arches joined to form a perfect circle. A blacksmith provides a tyre made of a big hoop of iron to precisely match the distance around the rim. You heat the metal tyre until it expands just enough to allow the wooden wheel to be eased on with a hammer. The tyre is then doused with water to shrink and bind the whole wheel. A wheel should last for 2-3000 miles.

You need to be physically strong and multi-skilled and get to know the many specialist tools that wheelwrights use such as mortise indexers and tennon augers.

- **How many wheelwrights are there?** Very few, because they only deal with traditional wheels.

- **Job prospects and pay** You need to establish a clientele with museums, individuals and carriage makers.

- **Start-up costs** If you are setting up on your own you will need tools and a workplace.

- **How old must you be?** There are no age limits, but if you want to study carpentry or smithing you need to satisfy college entrance or apprenticeship requirements.

- **Training** The best training comes from working alongside a practising wheelwright. However, blacksmith and carpentry training will also help. Read about the history of transport and wheels and visit museums and shows.

- **Qualifications** None needed.

Contacts: *The Worshipful Company of Blacksmiths*, The Clerk, 27 Cheyne Walk, Grange Park, London N21 1DB. Tel: 020-8364 1522; British Woodworkers Federation, Construction House, 56-64 Leonard Street, London EC2A 4QS. Tel: 020-7608 5050. Fax: 020-7608 5051.

See also: Blacksmith.
Find out about: Carpenter.

Wigmaker   £ £

If you like the idea of working with human hair but don't want to deal with hair attached to the heads of real people, then wig making is a possible career. Wig making is an old craft and good quality hair pieces are still in demand.

People of all ages need wigs and for many reasons - hair loss through illness, vanity, fashion, theatrical productions, religion, etc. Wigs are worn by actors, models, fashion dummies and many more. You might also make toupees for people who want to hide a receding hairline.

The best wigs are made from human hair carefully matched for colour. This is woven and knotted onto a specially made mount or base. The work is done by hand or machine. It can take a week to make one wig. Sometimes nylon is used and legal wigs are made of horsehair. These latter are particularly time-consuming to produce. You need to have nimble fingers, steady hands and a lot of patience.

Your workplace might be a small factory or workshop. But wig making is also a craft that can be practised at home. Usually wigmakers work for small companies and there are also theatrical wigmakers. You could specialise in making wigs for private clients or for clients recommended by hospitals if they need wigs on the NHS. Some unusual places require wigmakers too, Madame Tussaud's is one example.

Your job will not just entail making wigs but also maintaining and repairing them. You can specialise in one part of the process or make the whole wig from start to finish - that is measure, make, cut, form and style it. Making legal wigs is a specialism in its own right.

● **Job prospects and pay** The demand for natural wigs depends on the fashion. But there is always a need for wigs for theatres, the law and hospitals. Theatrical wigmakers can earn about £80 per day if self-employed.

● **Start-up costs** Equipment if you are self-employed.

● **How old must you be?** 16+

● **Training** You can train by getting on-the-job experience with experienced wigmakers and this is probably the best way. Sometimes wig companies or theatres that employ wigmakers offer apprenticeships or traineeships, but it can be hard to get a place. A number of colleges offer City and Guilds in wig making on a full- or part-time basis.

Contacts: *Hairdressing and Beauty Industry Authority.* Tel: 01302-380000; *Incorporated Guild of Hairdressers*, 24 Woodbridge Road, Guildford, Surrey GU1 1DY; *Guild of Hairdressers*, c/o The Syndicate Group of Companies, Syndicate House, 27/29 Westgate, Barnsley S70 2DJ. Tel: 01226-297083.

See also: Embroiderer.
Find out about: Hairdresser.

A writers' agent is more correctly called an authors' agent or literary agent. An agent represents a writer to the publisher, film companies, TV, etc, and endeavours to obtain the best price for the writers' efforts in the UK or abroad. The agent will negotiate and check contracts, chase up payments and generally try to deal with any problems that arise from a writers' work. Sometimes they even act as a shoulder to cry on!

The terms literary or author's agent is more often used because few agents deal with articles, poetry or other shorter or minor works. They might make an exception for a well known author. Some agents even become celebrities in their own right because of the amazing deals they have secured for their writers. However, most work is on a smaller scale, dealing with writers who will sell well but not become famous. A good agent can advise on career strategy too.

Agents take 10 per cent or more of their client's income from the writing they represent. The work is labour-intensive and it needs a lot of physical stamina, energy and patience.

• How many writers' agents are there?

There are 65 members of the *Association of Authors' Agents* and many more who are not listed.

• Job prospects and pay
You can start work as an agent from your home and be self-employed. You could start work as a minion to an agency, then work as an assistant or trainee agent and then set up on your own as a full agent. To be successful you need to acquire a good client list and sell it successfully. If you start on your own with unestablished authors, which is likely at first, it will take a long while to earn a living. Pay is variable, starting salaries for working for an agent or as a full agent in a company are low. Many agents are self-employed and some work part-time.

• Start-up costs
Basic office costs – but nil if you join an agency and work your way up.

• How old must you be?
There are no age restrictions.

• Training
You don't need to take any formal courses to become an agent. But you need to learn about copyright law, contract law, current industry standards, how the industry operates in your specialism, e.g. books, selling rights, what makes a good book, script, idea, etc, and how to get to know the main personnel in publishing. Usually you do this by working your way up in an agency or by working in related

areas such as a publisher's rights department and moving across. You can go on courses for such things as copyright law.

● **Qualifications** You do not need any specific qualifications.

Contacts: *Read An Author's Guide to Literary Agents* by Michael Legat for a useful view of what literary agents do.

See also: Typographer.
Find out about: Author, editor, publisher.

X-ray operator (diagnostic radiographer)
£ £ £ £ £

You do not have to be a doctor to be a valuable part of a hospital team. If you have ever had an x-ray taken at a hospital you will know that the x-ray operator (diagnostic radiographer) does an important job.

Diagnostic radiography is one of two career areas for radiographers - the other is radiotherapy in which you specialise in all aspects of cancer treatment. As a diagnostic radiographer you are trained in using x-ray machines and in a whole range of methods of diagnostic imaging such as ultrascan. You work with x-ray equipment and patients and act as a technical assistant to the radiologist (doctor). You produce the x-ray image and in doing so adjust the x-ray equipment, position the patients, decide upon the amount of x-rays to be used and assess the technical quality of the x-ray image. Newly qualified, you work in general imaging to gain experience of accident and emergency work. You will have to be on call so that a 24 hours a day service can be provided.

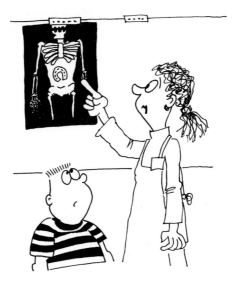

Safety is very important when working with radiation and that is why x-ray operators operate the machines from outside the room where the patient is.

You normally work in the hospital's x-ray department with advanced x-ray equipment and CT scanners. But you might also operate mobile x-ray equipment. Most radiographers work in hospitals.

● **Job prospects and pay** The job prospects are very good because of the high demand for trained radiographers in medicine, industry and research. There are opportunities within and outside the NHS. Once you start work there are several grades of radiographer which are gained once you have sufficient experience and expertise. You will earn about £13,000 as a new radiographer with the NHS and there is a formal career structure. A superintendent on grade one can earn about £27,900.

● **Start-up costs** None.

● **How old must you be?** Training is at degree level so you need to satisfy the age limits for university admission. You will not be accepted for training after the age of 50.

● **Training** Training is by degree course that provides in-depth academic study with professional training. Throughout the course you will do clinical training in hospitals.

● **Qualifications** Radiography is a degree level profession.

Contacts: *Society & College of Radiographers*, 2 Carriage Row, 183 Eversholt Street, London NW1 1BU. Tel: 020-7391 4500. Fax: 020-7391 4504. Website: **www.xray.demon.co.uk**; *British Institute of Radiography*, 36 Portland Place, London W1N 4AT. Tel: 020-7307 1400. Fax: 020-7307 1414. E-mail: admin@bir.org.uk. Website: **www.bir.org.uk**. Look at university handbooks in your local library to find out which offer radiography courses.

Youth hostel manager   £ £ – £ £ £ £ £

If you've ever enjoyed the hospitality of a Youth Hostel you will know that its welcoming atmosphere owes much to its staff. *The Youth Hostels Association* is the largest budget accommodation provider in England & Wales with over 230 Youth Hostels in some of the most beautiful countryside, town and city locations.

As a Youth Hostel Manager you will be responsible for the day to day running of the Hostel. Duties may included general reception/clerical work, catering, cleaning and the maintenance of the Hostel buildings and grounds. Depending on the size of the Hostel the position may include staff management.

This is a demanding position and you need to be confident, approachable and prepared to work unsociable shifts. The positions are full-time, although the YHA does have some Hostels which operate on a seasonal basis. Staff accommodation is available at the majority of Youth Hostels.

● **How many Youth Hostel Managers are there?** 230+

● **Job prospects and pay** Pay for Youth Hostel Managers is dependent on the size and location of the Hostel. There are good prospects for movement within the Association to different Hostels.

● **Start-up costs** None.

● **How old must you be?** To work in a Youth Hostel you must be 18 years old or over and below retirement age.

● **Training** Basic training includes Welcome Host qualifications and Basic Food Hygiene. There is also the chance to gain recognised NVQ qualifications in a variety of disciplines.

● **Qualifications** There are no particular educational qualifications necessary to become a Youth Hostel Manager although previous experience particularly in the Hospitality Industry is essential.

The best way to gain experience to be a Youth Hostel Manager is to become a General Assistant with the YHA. As well as gaining experience in every aspect of working in a Youth Hostel, as a General

Assistant you will have access to all internally advertised permanent vacancies which are circulated around the Hostels on a weekly basis.

Contacts: YHA recruits approximately 400 General Assistants each year to work from February/March through to September/October each year. For application details send an A4 SAE to The YHA National Recruitment Department, PO Box 11, Matlock, Derbyshire DE4 2XA.

External advertisements for Managerial vacancies are normally placed in newspapers local to the Hostel where there is a vacancy, or in *Caterer & Hotel Keeper* magazine. For further information write to The YHA National Recruitment Department, PO Box 11, Matlock, Derbyshire DE4 2XA.

See also: Listed building warden, housekeeper, butler.
Find out about: Bursar.

Zoo keeper   £ £ – £ £ £

By looking after animals in zoos you are helping zoos to do their job of conservation, education and the advancement of scientific studies. Animal welfare is one of the most important aspects maintaining a zoo. The umbrella organisation for zoos is the *Federation of Zoos*. This has 54 member collections which employ full and part-time staff.

Zoo keepers have many and varied daily tasks. You will have to clean and feed animal enclosures, prepare food, provide clean bedding, and keep enclosures at the correct temperature and humidity. You will help the vet care for animals that become ill or injured and record births and deaths. You will also help to devise ways of enhancing the animals' natural behaviour as well as dealing with the general public. Much of your work will involve talking to people not dealing with animals - you might talk to the public, owners, customers, and professionals. You might give talks and participate in and organise events and activities for school parties. You need to be keen to impart your enthusiasm and knowledge to the public.

Being a zoo keeper is not an easy job. You need to be prepared for hard manual work and long hours. Much of the work is routine. The work is often dirty and smelly. You cannot be sentimental. You might even have to humanely kill an animal. You need to be very patient because animals need long term attention.

This is not a 9 to 5 job so be prepared for long hours. You will often have to work at weekends and you will work longer hours during the summer. If you have an allergy to fur or fluff don't think about this job!

• **How many zoo keepers are there?** In 1993 about 3000 people were employed full-time in zoos.

- **Job prospects and pay** Jobs are scarce, but you will have better prospects if you have had experience of working with animals and have more than the minimum level of qualification. Pay is low, but some organisations might give you subsidised accommodation or the chance to work abroad. Promotion prospects beyond Senior Keeper are limited.

- **Start-up costs** None.

- **How old must you be?** Sixteen is the minimum recruiting age.

- **Training** Training is usually on the job and given by qualified members of staff. After six months probationary period most zoos will ask you to take a City and Guilds Certificate in Zoo Management (ZAMC) by distance learning through the *National Extension College*.

- **Qualifications** Entry requirements vary between zoos, but you would normally need five GCSEs including the natural sciences. Ideally you should have a high grade in biology, but chemistry, physics and maths are also useful. You would normally be expected to get your ZAMC after six months on the job. Some zoos require the Animal Management Certificate/Diploma or higher qualifications as minimum entry requirements.

Contacts: *The Federation of Zoos*, Zoological Gardens, Regent's Park, London NW1 4RY Tel: 020-7586 0230. Fax: 020-7722 4427. E-mail: cmlees@gn.apc.org; *Universities Federation for Animal Welfare* (IFAW), The Old School, Brewhouse Hill, Wheathampstead, Herts AL4 8AN; *Qualifications for Industry*, 80 Richardshaw Lane, Pudsey, Leeds LS28 6BN; *Association of British Wild Animal Keepers* (ABWAK), 12 Tackley Road, Bristol BS5 6UQ; *National Extension College*, 18 Brooklands Avenue, Cambridge CB2 2HN.
See also: Gamekeeper, falconer, shepherd, mobility instructor for guide dogs, bird sanctuary warden, ecologist.
Find out about: Health and safety officer.

Useful addresses. Find out about...

Actor *Equity (British Actor's Equity Association),* Guild House, Upper St Martins Lane, London WC2H 9EG. Tel: 020-7379 6000. Fax: 020-7379 7001. E-mail: info@equity.org.uk. Website: www.equity.org.uk

Alexander Technique teacher *The Professional Association of Alexander Teachers,* Steve Beech (Secretary) Tel: 01202-686429; *The Society of Teachers of the Alexander Technique,* Tel: 020-7351 0828. Website: www.stat.org.uk; General information website: www.alexandertechnique.com/question.htm

Architect *Royal Institute of British Architects (RIBA)*, 66 Portland Place, London W1N 6EE. Tel: 0891-234400.

Archivist *Society of Archivists*, 40 Northampton Road, London EC1R 0HB. Tel: 020-7278 8630. Website: www.archives.org.uk.

Aromatherapist *International Society of Professional Aromatherapists*, ISPA House, 82 Ashby Road, Hinckley, Leicestershire LE10 1SN. Tel: 01455-637987.

Art dealer *British Art Market Federation,*

10 Bury Street, London SW1Y 6AA.
Tel: 020-7839 7163. Fax: 020-7839 6599;
Society of London Art Dealers (SLAD), 91a
Jermyn Street, London SW1Y 6JB. Tel: 020-
7930 6137. Fax: 020-7321 0685. Website:
www.slad.org; LAPDA, *The Association of Art
& Antiques Dealers Ltd.*, 535 Kings Road,
London SW10 0SZ. Tel: 020-7823 3511. Fax:
020-7823 3522. E-mail: lapada@lapada.co.uk.

Artist Contact your local art schools, Higher
education collage or adult education college.

Author *The Society of Authors*, Drayton
Gardens, London SW10 9SB. Tel: 020-7373
6642. E-mail: authorsoc@writers.org.uk.
Website: www.writers.org.uk/society.

Biologist *Institute of Biology*, 20-22 Queensberry
Place, London SW7 2DZ. Tel: 020-7581 5530.

Bouncer Contact your local night-clubs and
hotels.

Budgie breeder *Budgerigar Society*, 49-53
Hazlewood Road, Northampton NN1 1LG.
Tel: 01604-624549. Fax: 01604-627108.
Website: www.webdoctor.uk.com/bs.

Builder *Chartered Institute of Building*,
Englemere, King's Ride, Ascot, Berkshire
SL5 7TB. Tel: 01344-630700.

Bursar *Independent Schools Bursars Association*
(ISBA), 5 Chapel Close, Basingstoke, Hants
RG24 7BY. Tel: 01256-330369. Fax: 01256-
330376.

Cabinet maker *British Woodworkers Federation*,
Construction House, 56-64 Leonard Street,
London EC2A 4QS. Tel: 020-7608 5050.
Fax: 020-7608 5051.

Cake maker Investigate cookery classes at
your local further education college or adult
education classes.

Carpenter *Institute of Carpenters*, 35
Hayworth Road, Sandiacre, Notts NG10
5LG. Tel: 0115-949 0641. Fax: 0115-9491664.
Website: www.central-office.co.uk/Central-
Office/IOC-0-Frames-index.htm.

Computer technician *British Computer
Society*, 1 Sandford Street, Swindon,
Wiltshire SN1 1HJ. Tel: 01793-417417. Fax:
01793-480270. E-mail: bcshq@bcs.org.uk.
Website: www.bcs.org.uk.

Computer programmer *Association of
Computer Professionals*, Kingsway House,
Wrotham Road, Gravesend, Kent 13 0AU.

Cookery writer Join the *NUJ* or *Society of
Authors* (see Journalist).

Copywriter *Institute of Copywriting (IOC)*,
Honeycombe House, Bagley, Wedmore,

Somerset BS28 4TD Tel: 01934-713563.
Fax: 01934-713492. Website:
www.dialspace.dial.pipex.com/town/lane/xxc54/
copy.htm.

Counsellor *British Association for Counselling
(BAC)*, 1 Regent Place, Rugby, Worcs CV21
2RJ. Tel: 01788-550899. Fax: 01788-562189.
E-mail: bac@bac.co.uk. Website:
www.counselling.co.uk.

Crime writer *Crime Writers' Association*, 60
Drayton Road, Kings Heath, Birmingham
B14 7LR.

Damp course installer *Nationwide
Association of Preserving Specialists*, 3 Cowper
Road, London SW19 1AA; *British Wood
Preserving & Dampproofing Association
(BWPDA)*, Building 6, The Office Village,
Romford Road, London E15 4EA.
Tel: 020-8519 2588. Fax: 020-85193444.
E-mail: admin@bwpda.co.uk. Website:
www.bwpda.co.uk.

Dental assistant *British Dental Association*,
64 Wimpole Street, London W1M 8AL. Tel:
020-7935 0875. Website:
www.bda-dentistry.org.uk.

Detective Contact your regional police force.

Doll maker *British Doll Artists Association*, 31
Braeside Crescent, Billinge, Wigan, Lancs
WN5 7PQ. Tel: 01744-894784.

Dressmaker Look for classes at your local
further education college.

Editor *Association of British Editors*,
Westminster Press, 8 Great New Street,
London EC4P 4ER Tel: 01480-492133.
Fax: 01480-492805.

Electrician *Institution of Electrical Engineers*,
Savoy Place, London WC2R 0BL. Tel: 020-
7240 1871. Fax: 020-7240 7735. E-mail: post-
master@iee.org.uk. Website: www.iee.org.uk.

Engineer *Institution of British Engineers*, Royal
Liver Building, 6 Hampton Place, Brighton
BN1 3DD. Tel: 01273-734274.

Environmental health officer *Chartered
Institute of Environmental Health*, Chadwick
Court, 15 Hatfields, London SE1 8DJ. Tel:
020-7928 6006. Fax: 020-7827 5866. E-mail:
cieh@dial.pipex.com. Website:
www.cieh.org.uk.

Farm worker Contact the *NFU* for your area.

Farmer *National Farmers' Union of England
and Wales (NFU)*, Agriculture house, 164
Shaftsbury Avenue, London WC2H 8HL.
Tel: 020-7331 7200. Fax: 020-7331 7313.
E-mail: nfu.centralservices@nfu.org.uk.

Website: www.nfu.org.uk/; *National Farmers' Union of Scotland (NFUS)*, Rural Centre, West Mains, Ingliston, Newbridge, West Lothian EH28 8LT. Tel: 0131-472 4000. Fax: 0131-472 4010; *Irish Farmers Association*, Irish Farm Centre, Naas Road, Bluebell, Dublin 12, Republic of Ireland. Tel: 353 (1)450 0266. Fax: 353 (1)455 1043. Website: www.iol.ie.~bbourke/IFA/ifa.htm; *National Federation of Young Farmers Clubs (England and Wales) (NFYFC)*, YFC Centre, National Agricultural Centre, Stoneleigh, Kenilworth, Warks CV8 2LG; *Scottish Association of Young Farmers Clubs (SAYFC),* Young Farmers Centre, Ingliston, Newbridge, Edinburgh EH28 8NG Tel: 0131-333 2445. Fax: 0131-333 2488. Website: www.sayfc.org/.

Garage mechanic Contact your local further education college.

Gardener *Professional Gardeners Guild (PGG)*, North Lodge, Upper Winchendon, Aylesbury, Bucks HP18 0ES. Tel: 01296-651957. Fax: 01296-651293.

Gas fitter *Institution of Gas Engineers*, 21 Portland Place, London W1N 3AF. Tel: 020-7636 6603.

Geographer *Royal Geographical Society* and *The Institute of British Geographers*, 1 Kensington Gore, London SW7 2AR. Tel: 020-7591 3000; *Royal Scottish Geographical Society*, Graham Hills Building, 40 George Street, Glasgow G1 1QE. Tel: 0141-552 3330.

Geologist *Geological Society*, Burlington House, Piccadilly, London W1V 0JU. Tel: 020-7434 9944; *Geologists' Association*, Burlington House, Piccadilly, London W1V 0JU. Tel: 020-7434 9298.

Glazier *National Federation of Glaziers*, 27 old Gloucester Street, WC1N 3AA. Tel: 020-7404 3099.

Glove maker *British Glove Association*, 138 Plumstead Common Road, London SE18 2UL. Tel: 020-8854 4691. Fax: 020-8317 1632.

Goat farmer *British Goat Society*, 34-36 Fore Street, Bovey Tracey, Newton Abbot, Devon TQ13 9AD. Tel: 01626-833168.

Goldsmith *Institute of Professional Goldsmiths*, 4 Cavendish Square, London W1M 0BX. Tel: 020-7499 0900. Fax: 020-7623 233; *National Association of Goldsmiths of Great Britain & Ireland (NAG)*, 78a Luke Street, London EC2A 4PY. Tel: 020-7613-4445. Fax: 020-7613 4450.

Gymnast *British Amateur Gymnastics Association (British Gymnastics),* Ford Hall, Lilleshall

National Sports Centre, Lilleshall, Newport, Shropshire TF10 9NB. Tel: 01952-820330. Fax: 01952-820326. E-mail: info@baga.co.uk. Website: baga.org.uk/index.shtml.

Hairdresser *Incorporated Guild of Hairdressers, Wigmakers & Perfumers*, Unit 8, Vulcan Road, MI Distribution Centre, Meadowhall, Sheffield, South Yorkshire S9 1EW. Tel: 0114-242 1560. Fax: 0112-242 1480.

Health and safety officer Contact your local authority.

Health visitor *UK Central Council for Nursing, Midwifery and Health Visiting*, 23 Portland Place, London W1N 4JT. Tel: 020-7637 7181.

Herb grower *Herb Society*, Deddington Hill Farm, Warmington, Banbury, Oxon OX17 1XB. Tel: 01245-692900. Fax: 01295-692905. E-mail: email@herbsociety.co.uk. Website: www.metalab.unc.edu/herbmed/HerbSociety/information.htm

Herbalists *International Register of Consultant Herbalists and Homeopaths (IRCHH)*, The Registrar, 32 King Edward Road, Swansea SA1 4LL. Tel/fax: 01792-655866 (£2 for prospectus).

Holiday camp compere Contact *Butlins*.

Illustrator *The Association of Illustrators*, First Floor, 32-38 Saffron Hill, London EC1N 8FN. Tel: 020-7831 7377. Fax: 020-7580 2338.

Interior designer *Institute of Professional Designers*, Piccotts End Farm, 117 Piccotts End Road, Hemel Hempstead, Herts HP1 3AV. Tel: 01442-245513. Website: www.ipdonline.com/index.htm

Inventor *British Guild of Inventors*, The Granary Studios, 301 New Mill Road, Brockholes, Huddersfield, West Yorkshire HD7 7AL. Tel: 01484-660366.

Journalist *National Union of Journalists (NUJ)*, Acorn House, 314-320 Gray's Inn Road, London WC1X 8DP. Tel: 020-7278 7916. Fax: 020-7837 8143. E-mail: nuj@mcr1.poptel.org.uk. Website: www.gn.apc.org/media/nuj.html

Landscape historian *Director of Studies*, Landscape, Heritage & Society, Department of History, Chester College of Higher Education, Parkgate Road, Chester CH1 4BJ. Tel: 01244-375444. Fax: 01244-392820. Website: www.chester.ac.uk (MA course).

Librarian *Career Development Group (formerly Association of Assistant Librarians),* c/o The Library Association, 7 Ridgmount Street, London WC1E 7AE. Tel: 020-76367543. Website: www.la-hq.org.uk.

Local government heritage officer Contact your local authority.

Make-up artist Investigate stage craft courses at colleges.

Marine biologist *Marine Biological Association of the UK,* Citadel Hill, Plymouth Pl1 2PB. Tel: 01752-633100.

Masseur/se *Institute of Massage and Movement (IMO),* 21 Tarnside Road, Orrell, Wigan, Lancs WN5 8RN. Tel/fax: 01695-623860; *Scottish Massage Therapists Organisation (SMTO),* 70 Lochside Road, Bridge of Don, Aberdeen AB23 8QW. Tel: 01224-822956. Fax: 01224-822960.

Model maker Ask at your local library for details of clubs near you and contact the *Guild of Master Craftsmen,* Castle Place, 166 High Street, Lewes, Sussex BN7 1XU.

MP Ask at your local library for information about political parties in your area.

Musician *Incorporated Society of Musicians,* 10 Stratford Place, London W1N 9AE. Tel: 020-7629 4413. Fax: 020-74081538. Website: www.ism.org.uk; *Royal Society of Musicians of Great Britain,* 10 Stratford Place, London W1N 9AE. Tel: 020-7629 6137.

Museum worker *Museums Association,* 42 Clerkenwell Close, London EC1R 0PA. Fax: 020-7250 1929. Website: www.museumsassociation.org.

Nurse *Royal College of Nursing,* 20 Cavendish Square, London W1M 0AB. Tel: 020-7409 3333.

Nutritionist *British Nutrition Foundation,* High Holborn House, 52-54 High Holborn, London WC1V 6RQ. Tel: 020-7404 6504. Website: www.nutrition.org.uk/mainmenu2.htm; *Nutrition Society,* 10 Cambridge Court, 210 Shepherds Bush Road, London W6 7NJ. Tel: 020-7602 0228. Website: www.nutsoc.org.uk/

Oil rig worker ask your local librarian for the addresses of the major oil companies.

Ornithologist *British Ornithologists' Union,* c/o The Natural History Museum, Akeman Street, Tring, Herts HP23 6AP. Tel: 01442-890080.

Osteopath *General Osteopathic Council,* Room 432, Premier House, 10 Greycoat Place, London SW1P 1SB. Tel: 020-7799 2442. Fax: 020-7799 2332. E-mail: gosc-uk@dial.pipex.com. Website: www.osteopathy.org.uk

Outdoor centre instructor *Outward Bound Trust,* Award House, 7-11 St Matthew Street, London SW1P 2JT. Tel: 020-7222 3059.

Palaeontologist *Paleantological Association,* Lapworth Museum, School of Earth Sciences, University of Birmingham, Birmingham B15 2TT. Tel: 0121-414 4173.

Palm reader *British Astrological and Psychic Society,* Robert Denholm House, Bletchingley Road, Nutfield, Surrey RH1 4HW. Tel: 01737-822071. E-mail: baps@tlpple.com

Pathologist *Royal College of Pathologists,* 2 Carlton House Terrace, London SW1Y 5AF. Tel: 020-7930 5863. Website: www.rcpath.org.contents.html

Photographer *British Institute of Professional Photography,* Fox Talbot House, Amwell End, Ware, Herts SG12 9HN. Tel: 01920-464011. Fax: 01920-487056. Website: www.bipp.com/

Physicist *Institute of Physics,* 76 Portland Place, London W1N 3DH. Tel: 020-7470 4800. Fax: 020-7470 4848. E-mail: physics@iop.org. Website: www.iop.org.

Physiotherapist *Chartered Society of Physiotherapy,* 14 Bedford Row, London WC1R 4ED. Tel: 020-7306 6682. Website: www.qmced.ac.uk/ph/phcsop.html

Pigeon racer *Royal Pigeon Racing Association (RPRA),* The Reddings, Cheltenham, Gloucestershire GL51 6RN. Tel: 01452-713529. Fax: 01452-857119.

Poet *Poetry Society,* 22 Betterton Street, London WC2H 9BU. Tel: 020-7420 9880. E-mail: poetrysco.@dial.pipex.com. Website: www.poetrysoc.com.

Police dog handler Contact your regional police force.

Police officer Contact your regional police force.

Postal worker Contact your local post office headquarters.

Printer *British Printing Federation,* 11 Bedford Row, London WC1R 4DX. Tel: 020-7242 6904.

Psychologist *British Psychological Society,* St Andrews House, 48 Princess Road East, Leicester LE1 7DR. Tel: 0116-254 9568. Website: www.bps.org.uk.

Public relations officer *Institute of Public Relations,* The Old Trading House, 15 Northburgh Street, London EC1V 0PR. Tel: 020-7253 5151.

Publisher *The Publishers Association,* 1 Kingsway, London WC2B 6XF. Tel: 020-7565 7474. Fax: 020-7836 4543. E-mail: mail@publishers.org.uk. Website: www.publishers.org.uk; *Independent Publishers Guild,* 25 Cambridge Road, Hampton, Middlesex TW12 2JL. Tel: 020-8979 0250. Fax: 020-8979 6393.

Radio journalist *The Radio Academy*, 5 Market Place, London W1N 7AH. Tel: 020-7255 2010. Fax: 020-7255 2029. E-mail: feedback@radacad.demon.co.uk.

RAF officer *Royal Air Force College*, Cranwell, Sleaford, Lincs NG34 8HB. Website: cranwell.raf.mod.uk/index.htm.

Receptionist Your local further education college will have information about suitable courses.

Record agent *Association of Genealogists and Record Agents (AGRA)*, 29 Badgers Close, Horsham, West Sussex RH12 5RU.

Restaurant owner *Restauranteurs Association of Great Britain (RAGB)*, 28 Kingsway, London WC2B 6JR. Tel: 020-7831 8727. Fax: 020-7831 8703.

Roofer *Institute of Roofing*, The Building Centre, 26 Stone Street, London WC1E 7BT. Tel: 020-7436 0103. Fax: 020-7636 1287.

Sailor *Britannia Royal Naval College*, Dartmouth, Devon TQ6 0HJ. Tel: 01803-832141.

Salesperson *Professional Salespersons Association (PSA)*, 22 Foxglove Lane, Chessington, Surrey KT9 1QB. Tel: 020-8391 9092. Fax: 020-8391 9375. E-mail: richardowers@compuserve.com.

Scientist Contact universities for details of science degrees.

Sea captain See Sailor.

Second-hand bookseller If you are going to sell more valuable and interesting books than simply second-hand paperbacks contact the *Antiquarian Booksellers Association*, Sackville House, 40 Piccadilly, London W1V 9PA. Tel: 020-7439 3118. Fax: 020-7439 3119.

Security guard Look in your local paper for jobs or contact firms directly.

Social worker *British Association of Social Workers*, 16 Kent Street, Birmingham BS1 6BY. Tel: 0121-622 3911. Website: www.basw.demon.co.uk

Solicitor *The General Council of the Bar*, 3 Bedford Row, London WC1R 4DB. Tel: 020-7242 0082.

Sports teacher *Loughborough University*, Loughborough, Leicestershire LE11 3TU. Tel: 01509-263171. Website: www.info.lboro.ac.uk/ Other colleges have specialist physical education teacher courses.

Surveyor *Royal Institution of Chartered Surveyors*, 12 Great George Street, London SW1P 3AD. Tel: 020-7222 7000. Website: www.rics.org.uk.

Tailor *Guild of Master Craftsmen*, Castle Place, 166 High Street, Lewes, Sussex BN7 1XU.

Tarot reader *British Astrological and Psychic Society*, Robert Denholm House, Bletchingley Road, Nutfield, Surrey RH1 4HW. Tel: 01737-822071. E-mail: baps@tlpple.com.

Taxi driver *National Taxi Association (NTA)*, 5 Clifton hill, Brighton, East Sussex BN1 3HL. Tel: 01273-729403. Fax: 01273-728122; *Society of Professional Licensed Taxi Drivers*, Mountview House, Lennox Road, London N4 3TY. Tel: 020-7281 7676. Fax: 020-7561 9775.

Teacher *National Union of Teachers (NUT)*, Hamilton House, Mabledon Place, London WC1H 9BD. Tel: 020-73886191. Website: www.teachers.org.uk/index.html

Technical illustrator *Association of Illustrators (AoI)*, 1st floor, Saffron Hill, London EC1N 8FN. Tel: 020-7831 7377. Fax: 020-7831 6277.

Traffic warden Contact your local police force.

Train driver *Transport and General Workers Union (TGWU)*, Transport House, 16 Palace Street, London SW1E 5JD. Tel: 020-7828 7788.

Vet *British Veterinary Association*, 7 Mansfield Street, London W1M 0AT. Tel: 020-7636 6541. Fax: 020-74362970. E-mail: bvahq@bva.org.uk. Website: www.bva.co.uk/; *Royal College of Veterinary Surgeons*, Belgravia House, 62-64 Horseferry Road, London SW1P 2AF. Tel: 020-7222 2001. Website: www.rcvs.org.uk.

Wood carver *British Woodcarvers Association (BWA)*, 25 Summerfield Drive, Nottage, Porthcawl, Glamorgan CF36 3PB. Tel/fax: 01656-786937. Website: www.woodworking.co.uk/html/bwa.html.

Woodworker *British Woodworkers Federation*, Construction House, 56-64 Leonard Street, London EC2A 4QS. Tel: 020-7608 5050. Fax: 020-7608 5051.

Writer *The Society of Authors*, Drayton Gardens, London SW10 9SB. Tel: 020-7373 6642. E-mail: authorsoc@writers.org.uk. Website: www.writers.org.uk/society

Youth Club leader *Youth Clubs UK*, 2nd Floor, Kirby House, 20-24 Kirby Street, London EC1N 8TS. Tel: 020-7242 4045. Website: www.youthclubs.org.uk/index.htm.

Further reading

An Author's Guide to Literary Agents by Michael Legat (Hale, 1995)

Astronomy Now, (Pole Star Publications, PO Box 175, Tonbridge, Kent TN10 4ZY)

Auction, Law & Practice by Brian Harvey and Franklin Meisel (OUP, 2nd edition)

The A-Z of Careers and Jobs edited by Diane Burston (Kogan Page, 8th edition, 1997)

British Archaeology (Council for British Archaeology, Bowes Morrell House, 111 Walmgate, York YO1 2UA)

Careers in Environmental Conservation by John McCormick (Kogan Page, 5th edition, 1992)

Careers in Landbased Industries (Warwickshire Careers Services, 10 Northgate Street, Warwick CV34 4SR)

Caterer & Hotel Keeper, Reed Business Information Ltd, Quadrant House, The Quadrant, Sutton, Surrey SM2 5AS)

CBA Briefing (Council for British Archaeology, Bowes Morrell House, 111 Walmgate, York YO1 2UA)

Chambers Crossword Manual by Don Manley (Chambers, 1992)

Directory of British Associations (CBD Research Ltd, annually)

Environmental Careers Handbook (Trotman)

Family Tree Magazine (61 Great Whyte, Hungtingdon, Cambridgeshire PE17 1HL)

Genealogist's Magazine (Society of Genealogists, 14 Charterhouse Buildings, Goswell Road, London EC1M 7BA)

How to Compile and Sell Crosswords and other Puzzles by Graham R Stevenson (Allison & Busby, 1997)

The Ivanhoe Career Guide to Patent Attorneys 1998 (Cambridge Market Intelligence Ltd with CIPA, London House, Parkgate Road, London SW11 4NQ)

Occupations 1999 edited by Peter Turvey (Careers and Occupational Information Centre, PO Box 289a, Thames Ditton, Surrey KT7 0ZS)

Offbeat Careers by Vivien Donald (Kogan Page, 3rd edition, 1995)

Research for Writers by Ann Hoffman (A&C Black, 4th edition, 1992)

Sponsorship for students (CRAC, annually)

Taxidermy - A complete manual by John Metcalf

University and College Entrance Official Guide (UCAS, annually)

Which University (Hobsons, annually)

Who's Who in the Environment by K Aldous and K Adatia (Environmental Council, 1995)

The Writer's Handbook edited by Barry Turner (Macmillan, annually)

Writers' & Artists' Yearbook edited (A&C Black, annually)